Celtic Carved Lovespoons

30 PATTERNS

Celtic Carved Lovespoons

30 PATTERNS

Sharon Littley & Clive Griffin

Fox
Chapel Publishing

1970 Broad Street • East Petersburg, PA 17520
www.FoxChapelPublishing.com

Celtic Carved Lovespoons is an original work, first published in 2002 by
The Guild of Master Craftsmen Publications Ltd. The Patterns contained
herein are copyrighted by the author. Artists may make up to three
photocopies of each individual pattern for personal use. The patterns
themselves, however, are not to be duplicated for resale or distribution under
any circumstances. This is a violation of copyright law.

Publisher: Alan Giagnocavo

Cover and finished project photography by Anthony Bailey, The Guild of
Master Craftsmen Photographic Studio.
Design by Chris Halls at Mind's Eye Design.
Cover design by GMC Publications Design Studio.
Illustrations by Toby Haynes from originals by Sharon Littley.

Thanks to the following for the kind loan of images produced in this book:
Brecknock Museum, Brecon, Powys, Wales, page 5; St. Fagan's Museum of
Welsh Life, Cardiff, Wales, pages 3 and 4 (copyright for which is held by the
National Museums and Galleries of Wales).

Special thanks to Ashley Iles Tools for their assistance with this book.

ISBN 1-56523-209-7

To order your copy of this book,
please send check or money order
for the cover price plus $3.50 shipping to:
Fox Chapel Publishing Company, Inc.
Book orders
1970 Broad St.
East Petersburg, PA 17520
Or visit us on the web at www.FoxChapelPublishing.com

Printed and bound by Kyodo Printing (Singapore) under the supervision
of MRM Graphics, Winslow, Buckinghamshire, UK

10 9 8 7 6 5 4 3 2

Because carving wood and other materials inherently includes the risk of
injury and damage, this book cannot guarantee that creating the projects in
this book is safe for everyone. For this reason, this book is also sold without
warranties or guaranties of any kind, express or implied, and the publisher and
author disclaim any liability for any injuries, losses or damages caused in any
way by the content of this book or the reader's use of the tools needed to
complete the projects presented here. The publisher and the author urge all
carvers to thoroughly review each project and to understand the use of all tools
before beginning any project.

DEDICATION

I dedicate this book to my late parents, Barbara and Eric Williams, who died aged 66 and 52 respectively. They were very special to me. I miss them both so much and hold their memories close to my heart. They gave me everything that makes me the person I am today: in love, skills and abilities, and much, much more. I am indebted to them both.

Thank you, Mam and Dad – one day we'll be together again and I'll see your smiling faces.

Sharon

To those who first thought of the idea, and to those that followed who have made the practice of lovespoon carving the tradition that it is today. It has allowed people like me to develop the skills and to pass on the custom to forthcoming generations.

Clive

ACKNOWLEDGEMENTS

This book has come about thanks to so many people – many of whom are unaware that they have been influential in helping us decide to publish this book. To list everyone who has been supportive is impossible, so to all our family and friends who have been with us all the way – friends in the British Woodcarvers' Association, those at the classes I teach, visitors to exhibitions and events, and everyone who gave us the extra push when we needed it – please accept this as a genuine thank you.

I am especially indebted to friends Pam Beall, Christine Gittins, Nicole Dobbin, Sandra Hapgood and Judith Bevan for their unfailing support, encouragement and guidance and, more importantly, for being at the end of the telephone when I have felt stressed, especially throughout the past year.

The information for this book was researched from many sources, and I would like to thank staff at the Museum of Welsh Life for their willing help.

Thanks go to Dewi Morris for emphasizing the need for a book such as this, and to Dick Onians for his ready encouragement when I was being asked to teach, for his support when I mentioned writing a book, and for giving me faith in my abilities.

Thanks also to the staff at The Guild of Master Craftsman Publications for coming up trumps in producing the creative and inspirational book that we so wanted published: to Kylie Johnston, our editor, who made working on the book a pleasure; to photographer Anthony Bailey; designer Chris Halls at Mind's Eye Design; and illustrator Toby Haynes.

I would also like to say a big thank you to Clive who made writing this book possible. Without him carving most of the patterns, this book may never have happened. It's been a pleasure to work with you, Clive, and I hope that you will now finally admit that it was not 'another hare-brained idea' – even if was hard graft!

I would also like to say thank you to Clive's wife, Mary, for not minding when he spent long periods working on the spoons. And last – but by no means least – I must say a very big thank you to my husband, Geoff, who has been a constant source of encouragement. He's had to put up with me when I've been preoccupied, tired and irritable and absent for long periods while doing some of the carving and typing the manuscript. Thank you both; I hope you feel that we've succeeded in what we set out to do.

Sharon Littley

CONTENTS

NOTE ON MEASUREMENTS

Please note that both imperial and metric equivalents are used in this book, with a preference for the imperial system. Where equivalents are given, readers should be aware that measurements in brackets may be rounded up or down to the nearest convenient equivalent – these are intended to be a guideline.

If in doubt about measurements cited in the text in relation to electrical equipment or hand tools – for example, chisels – contact the manufacturer or supplier for further information.

METRIC CONVERSION TABLE

inches to millimetres

inches	mm	inches	mm	inches	mm
⅛	3	9	229	30	762
¼	6	10	254	31	787
⅜	10	11	279	32	813
½	13	12	305	33	838
⅝	16	13	330	34	864
¾	19	14	356	35	889
⅞	22	15	381	36	914
1	25	16	406	37	940
1¼	32	17	432	38	965
1½	38	18	457	39	991
1¾	44	19	483	40	1016
2	51	20	508	41	1041
2½	64	21	533	42	1067
3	76	22	559	43	1092
3½	89	23	584	44	1118
4	102	24	610	45	1143
4½	114	25	635	46	1168
5	127	26	660	47	1194
6	152	27	686	48	1219

INTRODUCTION

This book is an answer to the frequent questions that we receive from carvers of all abilities about where lovespoon patterns and ideas might be obtained. Our response is that there are only a few publications relating to the history of lovespoon carving and these do not actually supply patterns, but, nonetheless, we give suggestions on where copies of books can be obtained. Invariably at this point, the person in question comments that he or she cannot draw which makes designing spoons difficult. The problem is a recurring one, so this is why we decided to write a book ourselves.

Clive and I have worked together for a number of years and we are a great partnership. I am able to design patterns whether they be for lovespoons or other styles of carving. I can see in my mind's eye exactly what needs to be done and how to achieve that end. Unfortunately, due to commitments, what I often cannot do is produce the work itself, and this is where Clive comes in. Apart from being a self-taught, competent lovespoon carver, Clive – like me – works to a high standard, and he has a little more time on his hands, so he has carved most of the spoons that feature in this book. At the same time, Clive will tell you that he is unable to draw – and this is where I come in. Apart from the fact that Clive is one of my wood sculpture students, he is also my best friend, so I am happy to design spoons for him, making sure to include whatever symbols he wants. On completion of the drawing, I explain my thinking on how the spoon should be carved and he then gets on with the execution. This works well as we are in constant touch with each other, and we are fortunate to be able to combine our strengths. Imagine if you could not do this. Think how difficult it would be to create a work of art without being able to visualize the finished article. This is what is needed: the ability to 'see three-dimensionally', especially when you only have a line drawing in front of you.

In order to help you interpret the designs, we include a diagram of each spoon – front as well as some side and top view profiles, together with a photograph of the finished item. The illustrations can be enlarged or reduced to suit your needs.

Feel free to adapt the designs, too. Our intention is that the designs are a starting point for creating your own unique works of art. In addition to the designs, we also include a section of symbol templates so that you can 'mix and match' your own designs. We can't provide one for every eventuality, but we have included one or two variations on the most common lovespoon symbols. Of the heart shapes, for example, there are cushioned, fretted and entwined designs to choose from.

While this book contains some historical background information, we did not want this to be its primary function. Its main aim is to be a practical book that can be taken up and put down as you wish, without losing the gist of a chapter. We do include information on choosing and using tools, finishing and sharpening techniques, etc., but we have tried to keep this as concise as possible in order to keep the information clear and accessible.

Finally, I hope that once you have read the book, you will agree that it addresses a real gap in the market, and that it opens up a whole new avenue for you to create your own lovespoon patterns.

Sharon Littley

THE TALE OF THE WELSH LOVESPOON

Picture this scene at the end of the day
When the farm boy is resting from cutting the hay.
Both tired and dusty, his mind would wander
To the girl of his dreams, who lived over yonder.

Too shy to talk and unable to write
How could he win her, think as he might.
On a cloudless night as he looked at the moon
It came into his head that he could carve her a spoon.

First came the hearts to say 'I love you'
Then came the bells to say 'Marry me, do'.
Each night thereafter, he'd look at the moon
And think of symbols to add to the spoon.

A horseshoe for luck and the joy it would bring
For hopefully now, she'll be wearing his ring.
The key says my heart is safely with you
And diamonds for the wealth they'll hope to accrue.

The twisted stem shows two lives becoming one
A wheel means he'll work to get it all done.
A flower shows love and affection
A shield means he'll offer protection.

The chain expresses together forever, my love
And the cross shows faith in the heavens above.
Balls in a cage he'll have to face,
One for each child they'll wish to embrace.

As he explains the story carved in the spoon
While stealing a kiss by the light of the moon.
He vowed then that he would pass on this gift
For others to follow and give love a lift.

And so it has passed from father to son
And four hundred years later, it is still being done.
So that tells the romance of the lovespoon
And what went on by the light of the moon.

Clive Griffin

A BRIEF HISTORY OF THE LOVESPOON

The origins of lovespoon carving are uncertain, mainly due to the difficulty of dating spoons, but it is an ancient craft and very old examples are found in Wales, as well as in Scandinavia, Brittany in France, and other European countries, all of which claim that the tradition originated with them. What we do know is that the earliest surviving lovespoon is dated to 1667 and is held in the collection of the Museum of Welsh Life, St Fagan's, Cardiff, where it is on public display (see Fig 1.1, left). This museum is dedicated to preserving the ethos of Welsh customs and traditions.

Fig 1.1. The oldest surviving lovespoon.

During the early years, lovespoon carving – or 'whittling' as it was also known – was a popular pastime. Men would spend their evenings carving household utensils and tools with a knife, whittling the shapes out of single billets of wood. The size and shape of spoons varied depending on their function: for example, a soup spoon would be long with a curved handle and a salt spoon would be quite small. Other tools used would have been a 'twca cam' (a curved blade with sharp sides and bottom edge), a draw knife, an axe and an adze (a tool with a blade and a wooden handle which is used to cut timber).

Wood was used because it was the cheapest and most readily available material – steel and similar materials were still centuries away. Sycamore was often used – for kitchen utensils, for example – because of its strength and because it has no smell which might otherwise

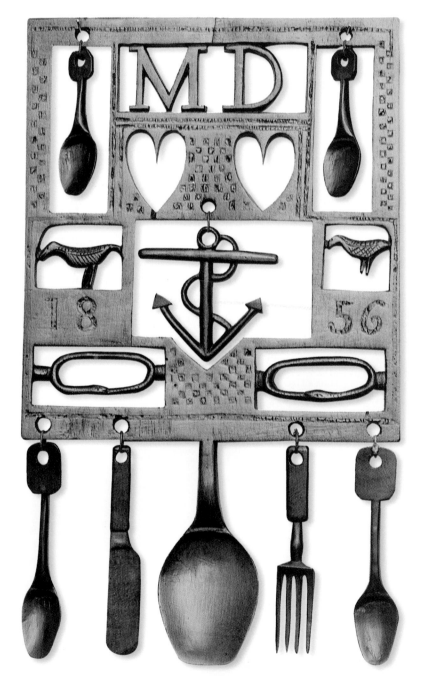

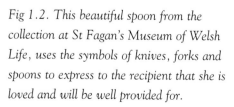

Fig 1.2. This beautiful spoon from the collection at St Fagan's Museum of Welsh Life, uses the symbols of knives, forks and spoons to express to the recipient that she is loved and will be well provided for.

taint food. As families increased their number, and in order to preserve skills and traditions, a father would teach his sons at an early age how to create these utensils so that they too would be able to provide for their family when it was time to set up their own homes.

As they grew up into young men, these boys soon discovered young women. More often than not, there would be competition for the attention of the girl of their dreams, so it became necessary to devise ways of winning her heart.

At some stage, the ritual of carving a spoon to do this began, and it didn't take long to evolve into a pre-courtship custom. As a youth carved a spoon, he hoped that it would convey the ardour of his affections and that it would be returned. If his amour accepted the spoon, she was agreeing to be 'courted' by him. The spoon would be treasured as a keepsake and hung on the wall for all to see. Indeed, the girl might have a number of spoons on display, indicating that she was not in a hurry to settle down. If a youth presented a plain, functional spoon you can imagine her reaction – it wouldn't have won her heart! The more elaborate and embellished the design, the more intense his feelings were considered to be. Soon the spoons became works of art (see Figs 1.2 and 1.3).

And so it is from these humble beginnings that the custom of giving lovespoons began. It is believed that the term to 'spoon' – an old-fashioned word which means to kiss and cuddle – has its roots in the custom.

Nowadays, lovespoons are given to celebrate many different occasions. They are given as wedding presents, for anniversaries, engagements and birthdays, but they continue to carry the same message and use the same symbols as centuries ago.

For today's carver, once a spoon has been commissioned, he or she endeavours to find out as much as possible about the person or the couple for whom the spoon is intended, so that

Fig 1.3. Bridal spoon inscribed with 'Mary Davies. Coed. Lland-y-vallog Vach. March 1st 1843'. It was donated by Miss Davies to Brecknock Museum, Brecon, Wales, in the 1930s.

the information can be incorporated into the design. To personalize the gift, a technique called pyrography can be used. Names, dates, initials and motifs can be burnt into the wood, making it a more precious gift.

LOVESPOON SYMBOLS
AND THEIR MEANINGS

This section lists the traditional symbols used in lovespoon carving and explanations as to what those symbols mean. I sourced a number of documents to draw up this list and while I am sure that other interpretations exist, it is quite comprehensive. This will ensure that you are conveying the appropriate message to the person for whom your spoon is intended. The symbols are listed alphabetically.

When you come to design your own spoons, please refer to the templates at the back of this book to help you create your own unique lovespoons (see pages 120–131).

ANCHOR

A sailor who spent a lot of time at sea often added the anchor to a lovespoon. It represents a desire to settle down, but can also mean a safe berth, i.e. home.

BALLS, SEEDS OR SPHERES

This means a desire to have children. The number of balls depicts the number of children. It also shows that love is cherished, and that the marriage will be blessed.

BELL

A bell represents the celebration of a wedding. These days it is also customary to include this on an anniversary spoon to celebrate the day when, years ago, the sound of pealing bells were heard all around pronouncing the happy couple as husband and wife.

BIRDS

The use of birds usually means lovebirds: the pleasure of being together and so in love. Sometimes doves are featured. These not only demonstrate that the couple are in love but also a wish for peace and tranquillity throughout their lives. A stork shows that the happy couple have been blessed with a new arrival to the family.

CHAINS AND LINKS

A chain made up of a number of links represents a wish to be joined together forever and that the couple's lives and destinies should never be separate.

Documentary evidence in a book entitled *Lovespoons and other Love Tokens*, displays a photograph of a spoon containing chains which it claims was carved in 1850 by a French prisoner in Lewes gaol, which has a dual meaning: that marriage is a 'life sentence'.

CLOVER

This represents a wish for good luck.

COAL AND SUGAR

These signify a wish that the couple never lack warmth or food. The coal represents warmth, and sugar sweetness or sustenance.

CROSS

The cross depicts faith in Christ. It is used to symbolize the sanctity of marriage and God's blessing.

DIAMONDS

Diamonds carved onto a lovespoon express a wish for wealth. It is not clear whether this means financial gain, or a more general desire for good fortune. It might be used to reassure the lucky girl that if she loves the man in question, she will be well looked after.

DOLPHIN

A sailor at sea, yearning to be home with his loved one, would often carve a dolphin to represent good luck. My own interpretation is that the free spirit is keen to keep in contact with those at home who have nurtured and protected him.

DOUBLE SPOON

Two bowls on a spoon represent a desire that the couple be linked together.

DRAGON

A dragon is a sign of strength and protection. It is also the national symbol of Wales.

FEATHERS

When the 'Prince of Wales' symbol (three feathers) or fleur-de-lis is carved on a spoon it not only represents the symbol of Wales, but expresses a desire to give service. Three feathers might also represent building a nest that can be called home.

FLOWERS

Generally, when flowers are carved onto a spoon they express affection and a wish for love to grow. A daffodil can also be the symbol of Wales and, for those of Welsh birth, it represents a recognition of one's affection for one's country.

FRUIT

Fruit expresses a hope for the fulfilment of love and of one's wishes.

HANDS

Hands express a desire for friendship.

HEARTS

A single heart demonstrates love and a desire to win the heart of the girl for whom the spoon is intended. Two hearts joined shows that love is returned and that the couple belong together or that 'two are as one'.

A heart-shaped bowl expresses a wish for a happy and fulfilling life together.

HORSESHOE

This is a common symbol used by many as a wish for good luck.

HOUSE

A house informs the girl of the carver's dreams that he is willing to work to provide a home and future for her.

GLASSES AND SPECTACLES

When seen on a spoon these represent a wish of the carver to see more of the girl, and also that he likes what he sees.

KEYS AND KEYHOLES

When a single key features on a spoon, it indicates that the girl has won the key to the boy's heart and to his home.

Crossed keys ask if the boy can win his girl's heart as she has won his. They can also mean a desire for security and a wish to share a home.

KNIFE, FORK AND SPOON

Cutlery means that the person for whom the spoon is intended will be well provided for.

KNOT

A knot demonstrates a wish to be joined together. For me, the never-ending Celtic knot means a love that lasts forever.

LANTERN

A lantern tells a girl that the carver would like to see more of her. In earlier periods, a lantern was used to ward off evil spirits, so an alternative meaning might be a wish to protect her.

LEEK

This is a symbol of Wales.

LOCK

A lock demonstrates a wish to lock the girl into his heart forever and to look after her.

LOVESPOON

A lovespoon conveys a desire for a relationship with someone special.

MIRROR

A piece of mirror on a spoon is used to avert the evil eye (a look that is supposed to have the power of inflicting harm) or to see the object of one's affection.

MULTIPLE SPOONS

These represent a wish for marriage and a family. Two spoons – or bowls – are usually larger and represent husband and wife. The others are generally smaller and are said to express a wish for the same number of children.

PEACOCK

This lets the intended know that the carver will always be alert to watch over loved ones.

SHIELD

A shield reassures the intended that the carver is willing to look after her and protect her.

SHIP

This symbolizes a sailor's desire for a safe return home to loved ones, and a wish for a smooth voyage through life.

SHIP'S WHEEL

Again, this demonstrates a safe journey through life.

SHOES AND BOOTS

Shoes and boots have been used as symbols for good luck since biblical times. Today, a shoe is often featured as part of the decoration of a wedding cake and boots or shoes are tied to the back of the wedding car. Both express a wish for good luck in the couple's marriage.

SOUL SIGN

Soul signs are usually fretted-out comma shapes and feature in pairs. They are ancient Egyptian symbols that represent the nostrils, through which the soul is believed to escape at death. In lovespoon carving, they mean 'I love you, heart and soul and I'd like our union to be sanctified'.

SPADE

A spade means 'I want to work for you'.

TWISTED STEM OR SPIRAL

Whenever these are featured they demonstrate two lives becoming one, or a lasting union.

TREES

A tree symbolizes growth and fertility. A tree might also symbolize strength and durability, expressing the carver's wish to be around for a long time to look after and care for his family.

VINE

This has the same symbolic meaning as the tree: growth and fertility. It shows that the carver has a sustainable love that needs to be nurtured.

WHEELS

Wheels were often carved by sailors or men who worked the land and represents the carver's desire to work hard for the girl of his dreams, and to steer her through life.

WHISTLE

A whistle expresses the carver's willingness to answer the needs of his loved one.

WINDOWS

These are used to display messages or to insert photographs, and express a desire to watch over a loved one.

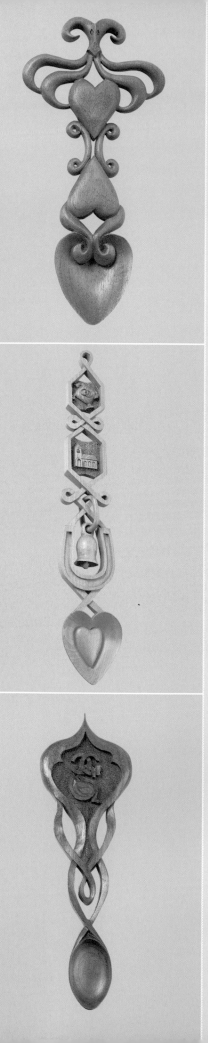

ESSENTIALS

EQUIPMENT AND HELPFUL AIDS

In this chapter we outline the basic tools and helpful aids that you need to carve lovespoons successfully. To keep costs to a minimum, we list only the most essential items that you will use regularly – and even then you can adapt your range by using less expensive, if a little more time-consuming alternatives. Some carvers are content to whittle away using only one or two knives, while others prefer a host of different-shaped chisels and electrical equipment to create their designs. Personally, I prefer to use chisels to do most of my shaping before switching to a knife to create the fine detail that is incorporated into my designs.

Hopefully, you will be proud of your finished product irrespective of the tools used, but it is always good to look at ways to improve on existing skills and knowledge, whatever level you are at. Once you have mastered the basic techniques and as your skills develop, you will become aware of other useful items and may wish to extend the range of your toolbox.

ELECTRICAL TOOLS

Before you begin work on carving your spoon, make sure you consider the safety implications of using electrical equipment. This is very important – all electrical items are potentially dangerous. Budget for safety items and buy them at the outset. For example, if you are using a flexishaft machine, you will need an apron, goggles and possibly a disposable respirator and, for many tasks, a dust mask (see page 17 for further details on protective wear). It is also a good idea to keep a first aid box in your workshop. If in doubt about the safety items you need, consult your local retailer or manufacturer's helpline. To reduce the chance of an accident, keep in mind the following safety tips:

- Carry out a safety check on equipment before you begin work and always have your safety guards in position when in use.

- Wear the appropriate safety gear.

- Make sure your work area is well-organized.

- Keep your hands away from blades – use a push stick if necessary.

- Make sure your clamps are secure during use.

- Do not work if you are tired or unwell.

- Avoid working when there are other distractions, especially if you are working at home.

SCROLL SAW (FRET SAW)

This is an essential piece of equipment (see Fig 3.1), particularly for the removal of waste wood in internal areas of your pattern, eg. when cutting out a Celtic knot pattern. An advantage of a scroll saw, especially with a fine-toothed blade, is that it allows you to follow – with relative ease – complicated twists

and turns that would be difficult to achieve with a conventional bandsaw. One drawback is that you can only cut to a maximum depth of 2in (51mm), although, in most cases, this should be ample.

Fig 3.1

BANDSAW

A bandsaw (see Fig 3.2) can be restrictive when cutting intricate areas because of the width and thickness of the blade. However, I find it extremely useful for shaping underneath a bowl and curving the top and bottom surfaces of a spoon, such as a curved handle (similar to the shape on a serving spoon or ladle).

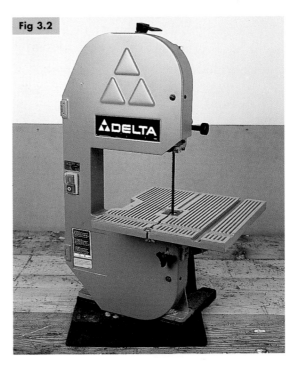

Fig 3.2

13

SANDER

A belt sander can speed up your finishing process and is useful for shaping the underneath of the spoon bowl, although I confess I don't own one (see Fig 3.3).

FLEXIBLE SHAFT MACHINE

This powerful motorized machine removes and shapes wood quickly (see Fig 3.4a). It is similar to the smaller hand-held Dremmel machine used by many hobby carvers but has the advantage of a long, flexible tube with hand pieces at the end into which burrs (Fig 3.4b), sanding drums (Fig 3.4c), cutters, etc., can be fitted. A flexishaft machine usually comes with a foot control which means you can work at your own speed. I use mine with a drum sander which makes sanding down large areas of work a quicker and easier task.

PILLAR DRILL

A pillar drill is the same as a hand drill except that it is mounted on a pillar frame (see Fig 3.5). Connected to the pillar is a small, level, movable surface on which to place your work, allowing the drill bit to enter the wood at precisely the right spot without it wandering. Since I began carving Celtic knots, this piece of equipment has become invaluable – a straight hole can be drilled into the tiniest of areas.

BENCH GRINDER (RUBBERIZED WHEEL)

This electrical sharpener is an essential tool for the workshop (see Fig 3.6). Some versions – the Ashley Iles, for example – come in left-handed versions or complete kits. For further details on grinders, see the section on sharpening techniques, page 46.

WHET WHEEL

Again, this is a very useful tool for sharpening blunt chisels (see Fig 3.7). I have only recently acquired one and it has quickly become invaluable. Whet wheels are not subject to heat build-up because water is continuously carried over the surface, keeping it cool. For more information, see the section on sharpening techniques beginning on page 46.

PYROGRAPHY MACHINE

A pyrography machine is not an essential piece of equipment, but it does have many uses (see Fig 3.8). It allows you to burn names, dates and other details that can enhance and personalize your spoon. It can also be used to add texture such as the speckled pattern on the Celtic knot section of the Mix and Match spoon (see page 106), and others. Some of the more expensive pyrography machines enable you to create the texture of fur or feathers without burning.

HAND TOOLS

COPING SAW

This hand-held saw (see Fig 3.9) can be used to cut away waste wood on external and internal areas. It entails a much slower process than using a scroll saw, but is a cheaper alternative. Extra packs of blades are available containing different-sized teeth per inch (*tpi*) for a coarser or finer cut.

KNIVES

Personally, I prefer to use a Swann Morton scalpel knife with a No. 3 handle and No. 11 blades (see Fig 3.9). Stanley supply a similar knife. They are available from most art and craft or DIY stores. Blades can be bought separately, usually in packs of five and, for a No. 3 handle, are numbered 10A, 11 or 15, each number having a different shape.

Lovespoon carvers also use penknives, Exacto knives and a Frost knife to list but a few. These are available from art and craft or DIY stores. Chip-carving knives are more specialist, having different-shaped blades for different cuts. These are available from specialist carving tool suppliers (see page 132).

Fig 3.3

Fig 3.4a

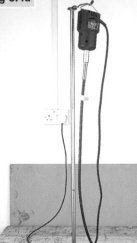

Fig 3.4b

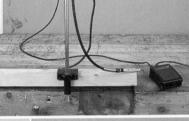

Fig 3.4c

Fig 3.5

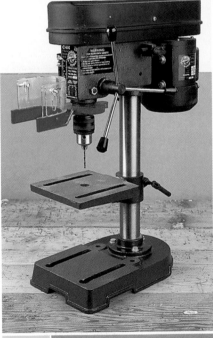

Fig 3.6

Fig 3.7

Fig 3.9

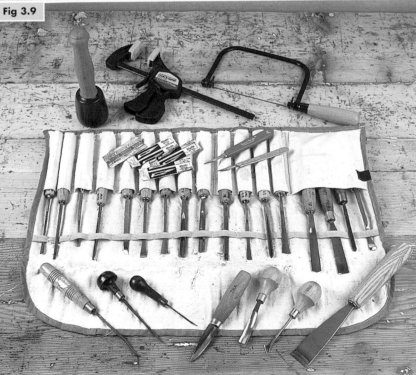

Fig 3.8

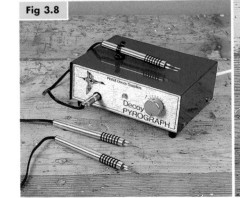

CHISELS

Chisels are available in different shapes and sizes (see Fig 3.9, page 15). There are straight, skew, fishtail, spoon-bent, long-bent, among others. Each one has its own specific function and each carver will have his or her preference in terms of brand. If you are about to buy chisels, I recommend seeking advice from fellow carvers to determine the best brand and then invest in one or two to begin with to see if you like them.

Once you have them, it is a good idea to regularly hone your chisels (i.e. buff them up on a leather strop or honing wheel) to maintain a sharp edge and maximize their lifespan. Each time you sharpen or grind, you wear away the metal and so reduce the longevity of the chisel.

NUMBERING SYSTEM

The most confusing aspect of buying chisels is understanding the numbering system. Every brand has its own, but they are broadly standard. The only difference occurs with the British numbering system. I use chisels made by Pfeil which is a Swiss company. A Pfeil skew chisel is listed as No. 1S, whereas the same tool in the British Ashley Iles catalogue is a No. 2. So, if ordering an Ashley Iles equivalent, always remember to add one number.

If a chisel is stamped with numbers 7/14 on the handle, the figure 7 indicates the depth of the curve which becomes deeper as the number increases, so a No. 1 is dead straight; a No. 7 is gently curved and a No. 11 is U-shaped. The number that appears after the oblique indicates the width of the blade. In our example, 14 means a cut directly into the wood measures 14mm from one corner edge to the other.

CHISEL SHAPES

Many carvers – especially professional carvers – use fishtail chisels. The flared ends allow easier access into awkward areas, and are finely balanced.

Straight chisels are very useful for beginners to carving. They have plenty of metal along the shank. If the edge snaps with too much pressure, they can be ground down again.

Spoon-bent and long-bent chisels are useful for hollowing out concave sections, such as the bowl of a spoon.

Skew chisels have a straight cutting edge with a 45° angle, i.e. one side is longer, with the corner edge forming a point at a 45° angle. The other side is shorter, with about a 135° angle. This chisel is extremely useful for awkward areas where only the point of a skew chisel will reach. I use the 1S/5 (1 refers to the straight cutting edge, the S means it is a skew chisel, and 5mm refers to the blade width).

BASIC CHISEL KIT

NUMBER	TYPE
1	Fishtail or straight-edge chisel
1S	Skew chisel
3, 5, 7	Fishtail or straight chisels
2, 8, 11	Straight chisels only
12	V tool
5L	Long-bent spoon
Scalpel handle No. 3	
Scalpel blades (No. 10A or 11 blades)	
A Frost knife	

I have not supplied details of specific blade widths – these will vary depending on what you carve – but the wider the cutting blade, the more wood it removes, and the smaller the blade, the easier it is to get into intricate areas. I advise you to include a couple of chisels with a 12mm or 14mm width and one or two with a 5mm width. Certainly, the most versatile tools in your kit will be two No. 3 chisels: such as ones with a 5mm and a 14mm cutting edge.

Please note that my chisels are available in metric measurements but, depending on the country of origin, some tools are supplied in imperial or in both metric and imperial.

Equivalents are provided in the conversion table (see page viii). Alternatively, please consult the manufacturer's catalogue.

HELPFUL AIDS
These household and workshop objects come in surprisingly useful as aids for many aspects of carving.

FLEXIBLE CURVE
This is useful for copying shapes from one side to another.

BOBBLE MAKER
This makes different-sized bobbles for babies' hats and is good to draw around for shaping chain links.

RUBBER MAT
Use this underneath your work to stop wood from slipping on the surface.

CLAMPS
These are useful for securing your work to the bench or when gluing wood, e.g. laminating pieces together (see Fig 3.9, page 15).

LEATHER STROP
A piece of wood sized 8 x 2in (20.3 x 5.1cm) to which leather is glued and compound applied (see Fig 3.10). Keep close to hand to strop chisels and knives – about every ten minutes. This will alleviate the need for regrinding.

PROTECTIVE WEAR
Use leather gloves if using the flexishaft. Leather gardening gloves are ideal as they fit the hand better, enabling more control when the article is held in the hand.

Buy special gloves for carving – they are coated so the chisel or knife won't cut your hand. They also have a snug fit.

If using a knife, it's a good idea to use thumb guards to stop the knife shredding your thumb.

Fig 3.10

These are available from specialist retail outlets or by mail order (see Pintail Carving, Suppliers and Further Sources of Information, page 132). Alternatively, you can cut the thumbs off an old pair of gloves and use these instead, which is just as effective. For a selection of protective gear, see Fig 3.11, below.

Fig 3.11

SCREWDRIVER
With a sharpened edge, you can use this as a chisel or knife.

UMBRELLA SPOKE
Cut into lengths, these can be ground down and sharpened to make the equivalent of a No. 10 or 11 chisel. They are ideal as a palm-held chisel and suitable for small work. Mine was given courtesy of friends Gill and Eric Avery of Oswestry.

SANDING AIDS

Use rasp files or rifflers to remove wood quickly, for example when shaping the underneath of the bowl. Pens, offcuts of wood and other items are also useful as aids (see Fig 3.12).

ARCHIMEDES DRILL

This is useful for drilling in those awkward areas where a hobby drill or flexishaft cannot reach. It is hand-held so that the angle of entry and the speed of work can be flexible.

MICRO DRILL BITS

Use these in conjunction with the Archimedes drill or a hobby drill. They are useful for carefully drilling the areas where chain links need to be separated, for example.

NAILS AND PUNCHES

Nails can be ground to thin points or rounded, and used to create different background textures. The end of an oboe nail can be cut off and, using a hacksaw, a series of vertical and horizontal lines cut into the metal to produce a grid-like effect. Used as a punch, it will produce a textured effect. (See Figs 3.13a, b, c, d and e for a range of shop-bought and home-made nails and punches.)

MODELLING TOOLS

These are available commercially or can be home-made to suit your requirements (see Fig 3.14). They are extremely useful tools for getting into tight, intricate areas when sanding.

SLIP STONES

Slip stones are really handy for removing burrs from the edges of your chisels. They are available in various shapes and sizes and can be used to suit most chisels (see Fig 3.16 for a teardrop-shaped slipstone). For further details on sharpening stones, see Sharpening Techniques, page 46.

CABINET SCRAPERS

These fine finishing tools are used to remove micro shavings of wood and come in various shapes and sizes. (See Fig 3.17 and also Questions and Answers, page 116.)

GLUE BOTTLE

I use a small transparent bottle with a metal-tipped, pinhead-sized nozzle so that the tiniest spot of glue can be applied. The bottle was originally sold as an aid to apply painted patterns for egg decoration, but similar bottles can be purchased from art and craft suppliers (see Fig 3.15).

COCKTAIL STICKS

After applying glue, use the tips of cocktail sticks to remove excess glue while work is being held or clamped (see Fig 3.15).

COTTON BUDS

Dampened cotton wool buds can also be used to remove excess glue.

SHAVING BRUSHES

After sanding work, the long bristles remove the fine sawdust that collects in all those nooks and crannies.

SHOE BRUSHES

Use these handy brushes to apply and remove wax when finishing work. Also use them to remove house dust and to freshen up spoons with dull appearances.

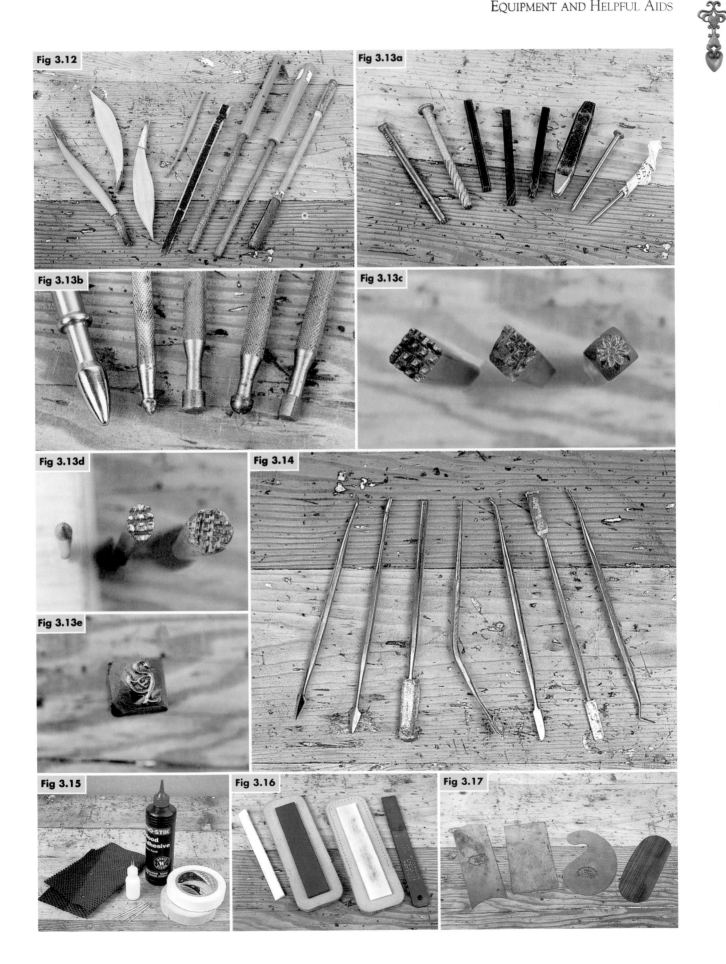

Fig 3.12

Fig 3.13a

Fig 3.13b

Fig 3.13c

Fig 3.13d

Fig 3.14

Fig 3.13e

Fig 3.15

Fig 3.16

Fig 3.17

GLOSSARY OF WOODS

Perhaps this is obvious, but the only material we use for carving lovespoons is wood. This section details the types of wood we have used for the spoons featured in this book (see Fig 4.1), and suggestions for other suitable woods for lovespoon carving.

Fig 4.1

(Clockwise, from top left) walnut, beech, cherry, yew, elm, burr elm, lime, jesmo, sweet chestnut, London plane and mahogany.

Wood is a living substance that has been used for household utensils, furniture and as an artistic medium for thousands of years. A tree is composed of three physical parts: the root system (for anchoring and absorbing nutrients), the trunk (to provide support and strength) and the crown (where the leaves convert water

and minerals into food). The trunk is made up of heartwood (the central darker and more stable part of a tree) and sapwood (this is the living portion of the trunk, which is lighter and softer in weight and colour, contains moisture or resins and is more subject to disease). It is made up of cell structures and fibres (which carry food and water) and is commonly referred to as grain. It is the grain that causes all sorts of difficulties for carvers and is one of the first things you learn to deal with when you start carving.

The best woods for carving are hardwoods. They are close-grained and will hold detail, but they are often more difficult to carve. They are stronger, more durable and will finish to a pleasing patina.

BEECH
Beech is a hard, close-grained wood that holds detail. It is hard to work, requiring patience, but is strong and durable for even the finest work.

BURR ELM
Burrs are wart-like growths found on trees such as elm. Within the growth, the grain twists in different directions making it completely irregular and difficult to carve but, once finished, the markings make the effort worthwhile.

I only use this wood for relatively plain designs to get the most from the colours and figure of the wood.

CHERRY

This is a hard fruitwood that takes fine detail. Its colour ranges from pale yellow to brown. It is quite pleasant to carve, but can be hard in places. Once polished, its appearance is transformed.

ELM

This is a tough hardwood and can often be difficult to carve. The colour varies from light to dark brown and the grain can sometimes appear interlocked and indistinct. The finish, however, makes it worth the effort as there is such a wonderful range of colours running through it.

EUCALYPTUS

This is hard to carve with a knife, but is strong and durable. It has a tendency to natural splitting that can appear at any time during the carving. Its colour is orangey brown.

JESMO (JOHN CROW)

This wood is similar to mahogany to work and can splinter. When carving with the grain it is a joy to work, but across the grain it proves difficult. I would not use it readily, but once finished, the rich colour is impressive.

LIME

This is an easy wood to carve with very little figure. Its close grain holds even the tiniest detail very well. It is even-textured and varies in colour depending on where it grows, from white to cream to yellowish pink. It is a good wood for beginners to carving.

LONDON PLANE

Commonly known as lacewood, this wood is pinkish in colour with a lovely ray figure that enhances any plain design. The wood is lovely to work but I have had pieces where the grain is interlocking and very difficult to work. However, I like the figure so much it is worth it.

MAHOGANY

The colour ranges from reddish to brown and is a medium-to-hard wood. It has a tendency to splinter, so take care working it. It can also have interlocking grain. When finishes are applied, it has a lovely rich patina.

MAPLE

This is a very hard wood to carve and reminds me of sycamore. It is close-grained with an even texture and holds detail very well. It is strong and heavy and ranges in colour from off-white to a light brown.

SWEET CHESTNUT

I have heard this wood referred to as 'poor man's oak' because the figure is similar. It is a pleasant wood to carve and holds detail well. Its colour varies and it has a light golden brown to yellowish appearance. I like using this wood.

WALNUT

This is a hard wood with tough, close-textured grain. It holds detail remarkably well. Its colours are rich, ranging from light to medium brown, dark violet and chocolate brown, depending on whether it is English or American walnut. I like using walnut for lovespoons and other carving, too.

YEW

This is a hard, fine-grained wood that is strong and durable. The heartwood colour ranges from pink to golden yellow or brownish red with a white sapwood. It splinters easily, takes detail, but can be difficult to carve, and has a tendency to follow the grain. It is difficult to acquire in large sizes. The effort is well worth it when the work is finished as it has a beautiful colour.

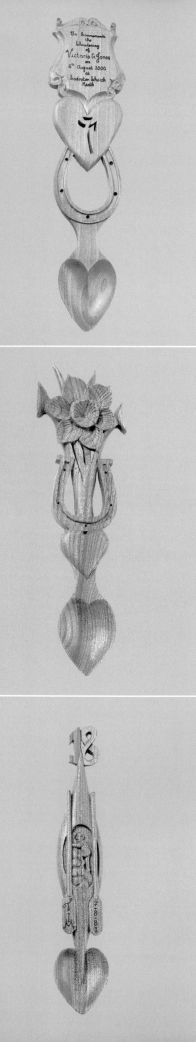

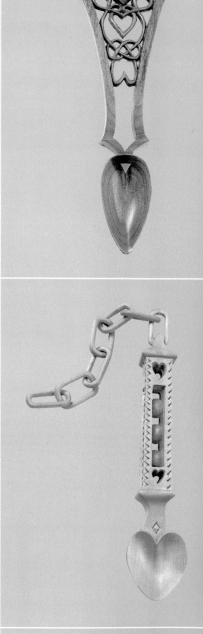

TECHNIQUES

CARVING
TECHNIQUES

This chapter explains how to carve a basic lovespoon, utilizing many of the techniques you will use when creating your first spoons, including how to work balls in a cage (sometimes referred to as 'seeds'), chains and spirals or barley twists. These techniques form the template for all the patterns in this book and will, I hope, encourage you to create your own unique designs.

TRANSFERRING A PATTERN

This is the first thing you must do. There are various methods of transferring a pattern to wood; see which you prefer, or use your own.

METHOD

1 Take a photocopy or a pattern copied onto tracing paper of your design and place it on the wood, securing it with masking tape.

2 Place a sheet of carbon paper under the pattern and then secure both sheets down on all sides using masking tape.

3 Use the point of a hard pencil or pen, trace over the lines of your pattern until covered.

4 Gently lift off the masking tape to check if everything is properly traced. If not, reposition and rework the necessary gaps. Some find this part tedious, but I like it.

ALTERNATIVE METHODS

1 Take a photocopy of your pattern. Using stick glue or white glue (Copydex), affix the sheet to the wood. Either of these products allow the paper to be lifted from the surface more easily than other adhesives. Ensure, though, that the glue covers the whole surface of the paper so that it doesn't come unstuck while using the scroll saw.

2 A tried-and-tested method. Rub pencil lead over the back of the lines of the design. Position your pattern onto the wood and trace over the lines. If there's enough carbon on the underside of your pattern, it will transfer the pattern like carbon paper.

3 Another way is to tape the pattern onto your wood. Using a fine point (a pin), prick holes through the lines until the whole pattern has been transferred to the wood. Using a pencil, join the dots together.

MAKING A STAB CUT

Also known as a 'stop cut', this type of cut makes it easy to remove sections of wood.

METHOD

1 To make a stab cut, hold your chisel at a 90° angle to the wood.

2 Holding this position, push the chisel into the wood to make a single definitive cut. Where necessary, stab cut across the grain first. This helps to stop the wood fibres separating as the chisel pushes into the wood.

CREATING TRIANGULAR RECESSES

METHOD

1 Make three cuts with a chisel: two stab cuts on the internal edge and a single cut along the outer edge, as follows:

2 Mark out triangles along the length.

3 Using a knife or No. 1 chisel – a straight-edged fishtail chisel is best – place one corner of the chisel at an angle at the internal point of the triangle, furthest from the edge of the wood. Stab the chisel into the wood so that it penetrates deep at this point and then lower it towards the outer edge, lowering the opposite end of the blade so that it severs the fibres at the outer edge.

4 Repeat on the other side of the triangle.

5 Next, using a knife, fishtail or skew chisel, remove the wood from within the two cuts. To do so, hold the chisel at an angle, with the chisel edge approximately 45° to the wood, so that as the blade enters the wood, it follows the stab cut already made, getting gradually deeper as it moves towards the point of the triangle, thus removing the wood chip in a single, clean cut.

CARVING A BASIC SPOON

Clive designed the pattern for this spoon while waiting for me to open up a woodcarving exhibition by the Welsh regional branch of the British Woodcarvers' Association.

Of all the spoons we have carved – many of which feature in this book – we both feel that this is an ideal pattern to show the beginner how to carve a basic lovespoon.

The good thing, too, about this pattern (and the others which follow in the Patterns chapter, see page 54) is that it is flexible enough for you to enlarge or reduce to suit your requirements.

Take care where the tail overhangs the end of the horseshoe. Because of the short grain here, it is liable to break.

Take care where the beaks meet. It is better to carve these with a scalpel or knife as the area is quite narrow to work in. Try to shape them so that they are wider where they join the head, narrowing towards the tip of the beak.

For a nicely cushioned heart, round the hearts well over the whole area, rather than just at the edges. It is best to use a piece of wood at least ¾in (19mm) thick.

Chip carve around the arms connecting the bowl and the hearts. You can use a No. 8/7 or 8/10 for this effect or create some recessed triangles.

SIZE
11 x 3 x ¾in (279 x 76 x19mm)
TYPE OF WOOD
Lime
SYMBOLS AND MEANINGS
Lovebirds represent the love between two people.
The horseshoe symbolizes good luck.
Entwined hearts demonstrate a love that is given and returned.

METHOD

1 Transfer the design onto your piece of wood using your preferred method (see Fig 5.1).

2 Shade in the internal areas of wood that need to be removed. Drill a hole into each shaded area leaving room to feed through a scroll saw or coping saw blade to cut away waste wood (Fig 5.2).

3 Using a scroll saw or coping saw, cut around the outside lines carefully to remove the external waste wood. Then cut out all the internal waste wood (Fig 5.3). If possible, cut each side out in one go and keep these pieces for later – you will need them to act as a 'cradle' or guide when cutting the side profile (Fig 5.4).

4 Turn the spoon on its side. From the top, at the birds' heads, mark a line 5mm (³⁄₁₆in) in from the left- and right-hand sides down to the bottom of the horseshoe. The cushioned hearts are marked so that both sides curve from the marked lines at the base of the horseshoe towards the outer edges of the heart and then taper back in towards the V at the bottom. The connecting arms between the hearts and the bowl are curved and need to be drawn as shown in Fig 5.5. Draw in a rough outline for the shape of the bowl.

5 Cut out the shape. Reposition the spoon into its offcut, securing it in place with masking tape, ensuring that you keep the marked out side uppermost, then cut out the shape with a bandsaw (Fig 5.6, page 28).

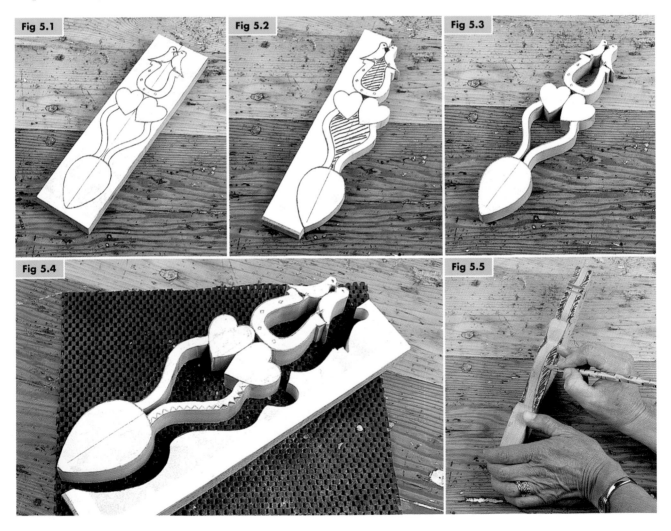

Fig 5.1
Fig 5.2
Fig 5.3
Fig 5.4
Fig 5.5

(On its side, the wood is wider than the jaws of the scroll saw.) You can also use a chisel.

6   Begin carving. Round the hearts at the top and sides (Fig 5.7). Keep the central area of the heart as a high point, tapering from the centre section down to the tip until cushion-like. Repeat with the other heart. They should be sufficiently rounded at the top so that the baseline of the horseshoe sits proud of the curved arcs, as if resting on them (Fig 5.8).

Note: a high point refers to the area where very little wood is removed, where it appears literally higher than the rest of the carving. A low point is where the most wood is removed.

7   Shape the spoon bowl. Use a palm-held long-bent chisel here, or a conventional long-bent or straight-edged gouge. To shape the bowl, remove wood from the central area, working towards the outer edges as the hollow gets deeper and wider.

8   To form the heart-shaped section within the bowl, start at the top right-hand side (with the gouge angled at about 40° to the edge of the wood) push the gouge through the wood, following the shape of the marked line. A vertical line should form at the section where the left and right curves meet at the V area (Figs 5.9 and 5.10). Work these areas so the curves naturally blend into shape.

9   Shape the underneath section of the bowl (Figs 5.11 and 5.12). Be careful to maintain a consistent line and thickness with the inside of the bowl as you remove wood. As a guide, use your fingers underneath the bowl and place your thumb inside to gauge the overall depth of the wood. If it is not consistent, remove wood from the thicker areas, but be careful not to remove too much – you might end up with a hole.

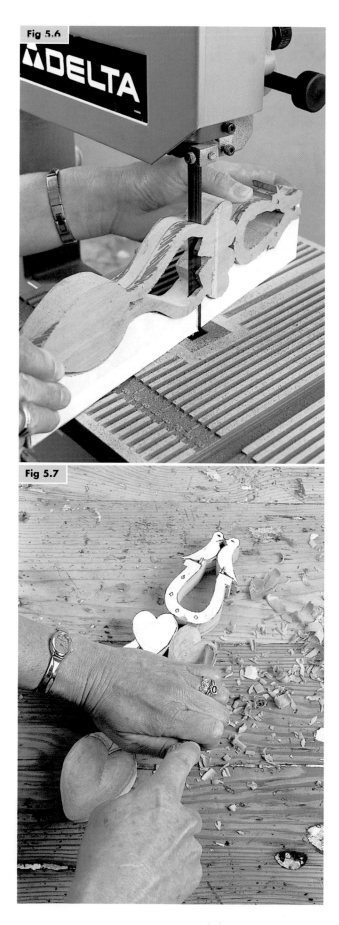

Fig 5.6

Fig 5.7

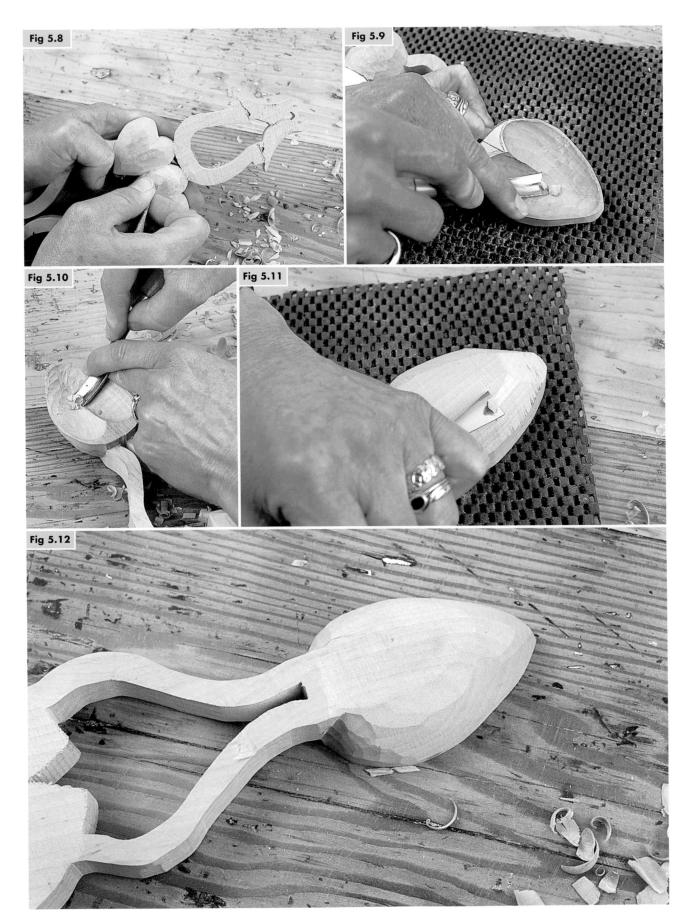

Fig 5.8

Fig 5.9

Fig 5.10

Fig 5.11

Fig 5.12

10 For added realism, drill holes or punch a nail into the horseshoe – on average there are seven nail holes in the U shape of a horseshoe, though we have used only six on this spoon (see Fig 5.14).

11 Next, shape the birds. Round the body of both birds by removing the square edges all round (see Figs 5.13 and 5.14). Shape the section from the head to neck so that the head becomes round, then shape from the neck towards the chest of both birds, down to the tail. As you shape the legs, take care not to break them. Use a nail rounded at the end to punch an eye, or burn an eye using a pyrography machine.

12 Sand your spoon starting with 180 grit sandpaper, working through 240 and 320 and, when it is ready for a finer paper, 400 or 600 grit (Figs 5.15 and 5.16). For a better finish, remove the backing paper.

13 Chip-carve the connecting arms using a No. 9, 10 or 11 gouge at an angle of about 45° to the wood. Remove the wood (Fig 5.17) or by carving triangular recesses (see Fig 5.18 and page 25).

14 Once satisfied with the carving and sanding of the spoon, finish with two coats of sanding sealer (Fig 5.19) and two coats of liquid wax (see Fig 5.20 and page 42).

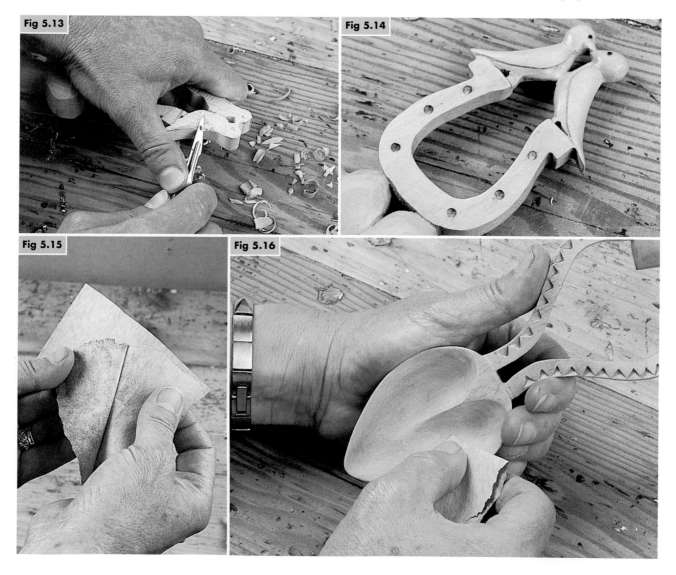

Fig 5.13

Fig 5.14

Fig 5.15

Fig 5.16

Fig 5.17

Fig 5.18

Fig 5.19

Fig 5.20

BALLS IN A CAGE

It is best to work a practice piece first, but if you want to make a start on a spoon design, give lots of thought to the practical application of your design. Decide how many balls you intend to carve as this will determine the length of your cage. And consider the measurements of the wood – there is no point designing a cage 1in (25mm) square if your chosen piece of wood is only ¾in (19mm).

It is impossible to recommend precisely how much waste wood to remove as this depends on your design, so what follows is a guide to technique only. The dimensions of our design are 1⅛ x 1⅛ x 2¾in (28 x 28 x 70mm), but if yours varies, you must adjust the width of the pillars as necessary.

METHOD

1   First transfer your design to the piece of wood (Fig 5.21). On all four sides, draw lines to mark out the rectangular cage that will hold the balls in place. The cage is made up of four pillars and each one measures approximately ⁵⁄₁₆in (7mm) wide x 2in (51mm) long. Starting ⅜in (10mm) from the top end of the block, draw a parallel line ⁵⁄₁₆in (7mm) in from one edge along the length of the wood and 2in (51mm) long. Repeat this at every corner. There should be two lines drawn on each face. The ⅜in (10mm) area without lines at the top and bottom end of the block needs to be drawn so as to connect the width of the wood to form a rectangle. Repeat this on each of the remaining three faces.

2   Next draw in the balls themselves (Fig 5.22). Draw the balls larger than the internal area of the rectangle so that the circumference overlaps the edges of the pillars. Ensure, too, that a space is left between each ball to make separating them easier. Having completed one face, repeat for the remaining

three sides, ensuring that the top and bottom of the balls line up on all four sides (Fig 5.23).

3   Starting inside the rectangular areas, remove the waste wood by making vertical stab cuts along all marked lines (Fig 5.24). Remove the wood from each section to end up with a flat surface approximately ⅛–¼in (3–6mm) deeper than the surface – about two thirds of the width of the pillars (Fig 5.25). At this stage you should notice that the pillars are being formed and that most of the circles you have drawn have been carved away, leaving only the outer circumference of each ball visible on the pillars.

4   Redraw the circles. The remaining lines of the circles left on the pillars will provide a guide (Figs 5.26a and b).

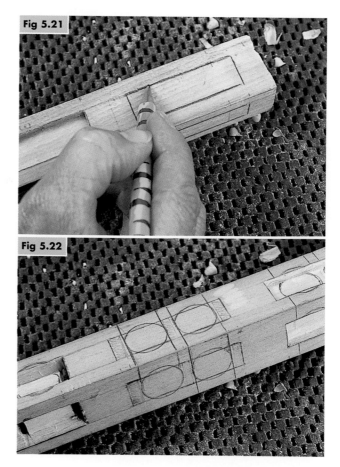

Fig 5.21

Fig 5.22

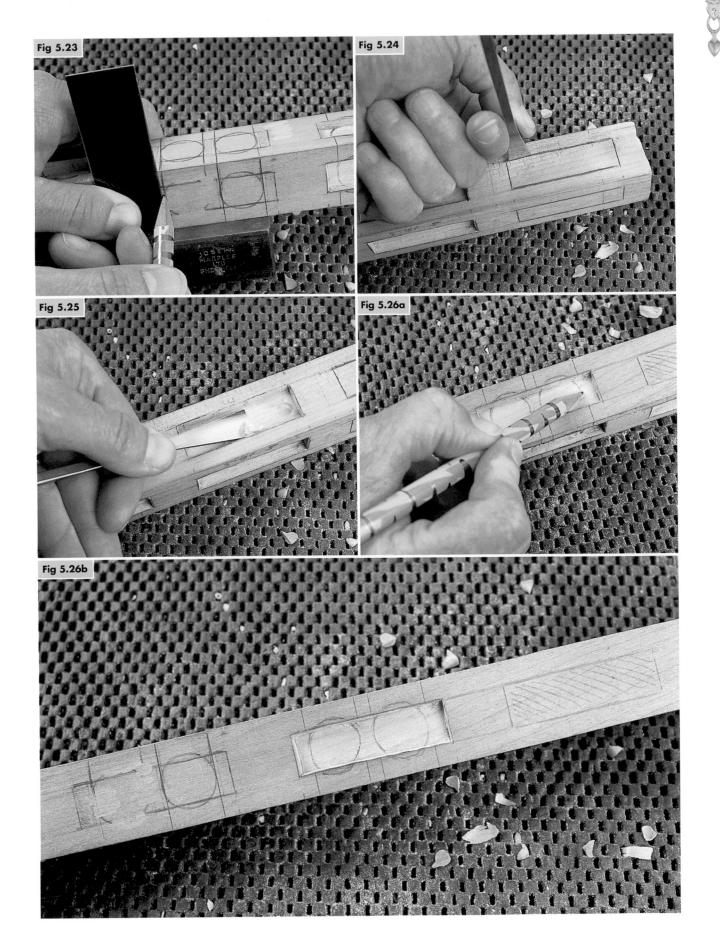

Fig 5.23

Fig 5.24

Fig 5.25

Fig 5.26a

Fig 5.26b

5 Remove waste wood from above and below the ball section. Shade the area to be removed (Fig 5.27), and then begin taking away the wood. It is much easier and quicker to do this with a pillar drill. Drill several holes through the shaded areas on all sides (Fig 5.28), then use a chisel or knife to remove any remaining wood (Fig 5.29).

6 Begin to transform the square into a ball. Curve the area of wood from the centre towards each edge (where the ball joins the pillar) (Fig 5.30). The curve should be shallow on the top section of the ball becoming gradually steeper as it approaches the pillar. Repeat on the other sides. Ensure that you maintain a consistent curve, so that as each section meets at the pillar, they form a continuous line around all four sides. Do not attempt to separate the sides of the balls from the pillars at this stage.

7 Having completed the sides of the ball, it is now time to work on the top and bottom of each section. Use the same method as above: work a shallow curve on the central area of the ball, gradually becoming steeper as it approaches the top and bottom ends. You will notice that as you continue shaping there is less wood attached to the pillar as the ball begins to become round (Figs 5.31 and 5.32).

8 Once the balls are circular and still attached to all four pillars, you can sand them (Fig 5.33). If you prefer a natural look, leave them unsanded.

9 Once sanded, separate the balls. Do this by gradually cutting away the wood in the same manner as before until they are finally loose and turn freely within the cage (Fig 5.34).

10 Clean up the unsightly cut on the internal edges of the pillars using either sandpaper or

a straight-edged chisel, a sliver of wood at a time. Be careful not to remove too much in case the balls fall out.

11 Balls in a cage can be executed in more complex shapes than a rectangle, like the hexagon, opposite (Fig 5.35).

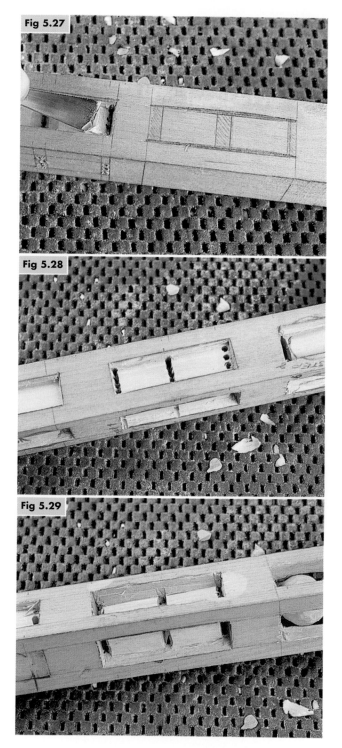

Fig 5.27

Fig 5.28

Fig 5.29

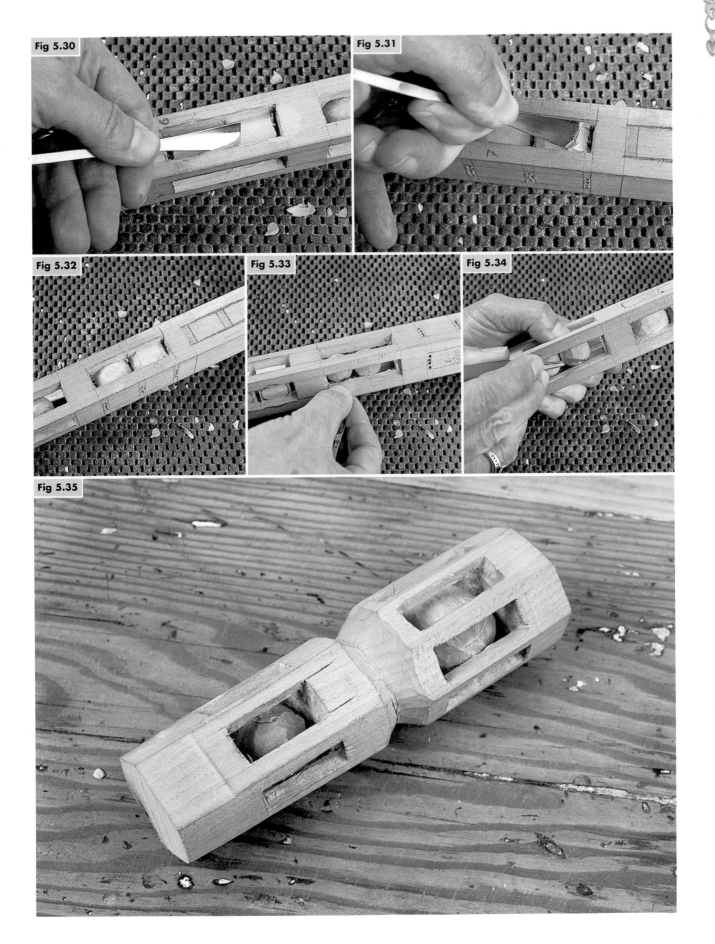

Fig 5.30

Fig 5.31

Fig 5.32

Fig 5.33

Fig 5.34

Fig 5.35

CHAINS AND LINKS

Like the balls in a cage, links or chains are carved from a single piece of wood. They look more complicated than they are, but do require a systematic approach and patience.

Give prior thought as to how many links you want to carve, and what shape you would like them to be. For circular or oval links, you need a square block of wood, but for the latter you will need to draw more elongated shapes.

Chains are traditionally featured at the top of a spoon, but they can be included anywhere in the design providing that you make allowances in your pattern for their position, and when cutting out the wood.

Our piece was carved from a waste piece of mahogany, which is not the best choice of wood, but looks quite good as the finished article. The block of wood measured 1½in (38mm) square by 24in (610mm) long which was cut into sections to make the method easier to follow.

METHOD

1 Draw two parallel lines approximately ¼in (6mm) apart down the centre of your block of wood (depending on the width of your wood, these lines can be wider or narrower) (see Fig 5.36). The gap between these two lines forms one of the pillars. Repeat the same method with the remaining three sides.

2 Shade the left- and right-hand margins of all four sides, i.e. from the drawn line to the outer edge, leaving the area between the parallel lines blank (Fig 5.37).

3 Remove the waste wood from the shaded areas by making stab cuts along the lines (Fig 5.38) then, using a chisel or router, remove the wood from the top surface until it is level with the top line on each side (Fig 5.39). This forms the central pillar. Repeat this method along the remaining

three sides until there are four pillars all joined at the centre. Viewed from the front, the shape should resemble a cross, about the same proportions as the Red Cross or first aid symbols (Fig 5.40).

4 At this stage, sand along the length of each pillar, ready to draw the chains in position.

5 To draw the chain sections onto the wood, first look at your spoon from the front, then draw your links onto each side of the centre pillar (Fig 5.41). Make sure that both the top and bottom lines match on each side of the pillar.

6 Next, turn the spoon on its side and repeat the method so that they start midway between the links drawn in the previous step. They should begin to look as though they will eventually interlock (Fig 5.42). When doing this make sure that the inner line of the horizontal link isn't touching the inner line of the vertical link as a gap is required to make the separation of links easier. Shading in the internal area to be removed may help you when you reach step 8. Alternatively, transfer the chain pattern by photocopying those that are already drawn, cut out the appropriate sections and stick them onto the remaining sides, again ensuring the lines on each side of the central pillar align correctly.

7 Cut around the outer shapes using a scroll or coping saw (Fig 5.43). Alternatively, cut out the shape using a knife – but this will take you much longer.

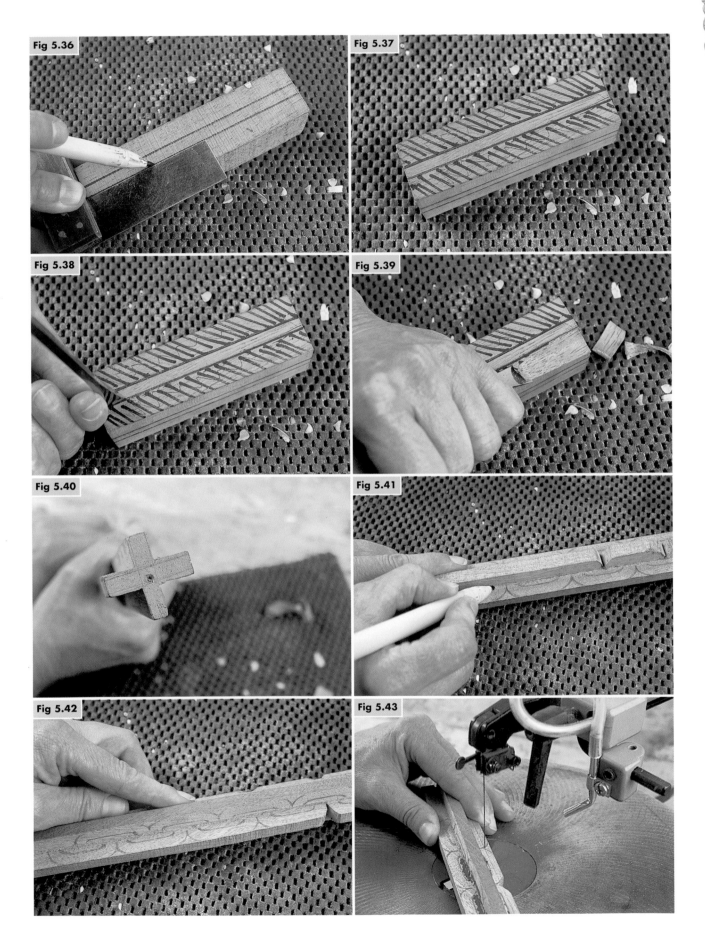

Fig 5.36

Fig 5.37

Fig 5.38

Fig 5.39

Fig 5.40

Fig 5.41

Fig 5.42

Fig 5.43

8 Begin to remove the waste wood. First drill a hole through each shaded area (Fig 5.44) and remove this section using a scroll or coping saw (Fig 5.45). Alternatively, drill multiple holes close together and remove any remaining wood with a knife or chisel (Fig 5.46).

8 Next, separate the section between the inner and outer lines of each link. Do this either by using a scalpel knife (Fig 5.47) to carefully chip the wood away until the chain separates, or use a mini drill with a very fine drill bit. If you choose the latter, keep the drill in line with the wood to be removed in order to alleviate the possibility of drilling into the actual link section. Repeat this until all links are separated.

9 Using a knife, keyhole saw or an old coping saw blade, gently saw between the outer rounded ends of both links to complete the separation process.

10 The links at this stage are quite crude, so use a knife to shape the links and reduce the thickness of wood to a more consistent and appropriate size (Figs 5.48 and 5.49).

11 Once satisfied with the shape, sand each link(Fig 5.50). Finish with shellac and/or wax (Fig 5.51).

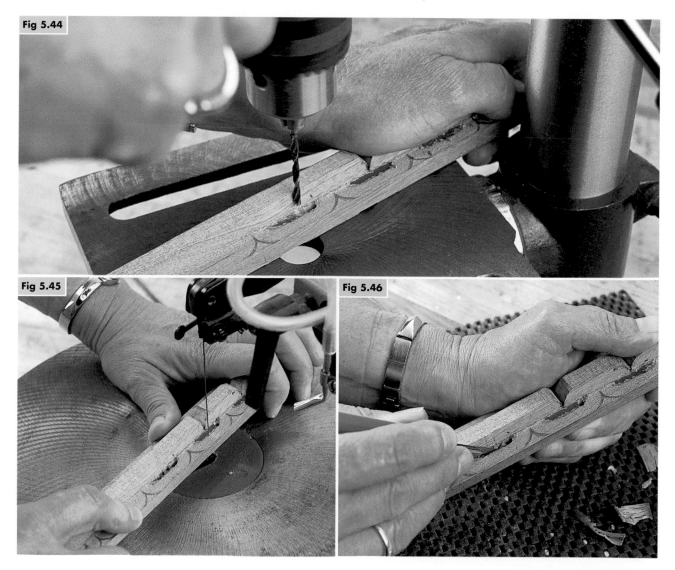

Fig 5.44

Fig 5.45

Fig 5.46

Fig 5.47

Fig 5.48

Fig 5.49

Fig 5.50

Fig 5.51

SPIRAL (OR BARLEY) TWISTS

Spirals or barley twists form an effective decorative addition to a spoon, and can be carved with concave or convex twists.

A concave twist gives a fluted effect, i.e. a U-shaped hollow in the valley and a peak at the high point, whereas a convex twist forms a V at the valley and a dome at the high point. The piece featured here has a concave twist.

As before with design elements like chains and links, plan the number of twists you would like in advance, as this has a bearing on the length of wood you need for this section. If you want a tighter twist (more twists in the spiral), you need to mark your wood out in square sections, whereas fewer twists need to be marked out in oblong sections. For our piece, the depth of wood was ½in (13mm) so we made the width ½in (13mm) to form a square section.

Note: there are two separate stems connecting the spiral to the bowl of the spoon. You need a minimum of two to form a spiral or barley twist, but more can be included if desired.

METHOD

1 Starting at the rim of the bowl, mark in a series of horizontal lines at ½in (13mm) intervals along the length of wood (if your wood is deeper than ½in (13mm), mark your lines the same distance apart as the depth of your wood (see Fig 5.52). Continue to mark these lines around all four sides (Fig 5.53).

2 Draw in a diagonal line from the bottom to the top corner in each of the boxes – these can be from top to bottom, left to right or vice versa (Fig 5.54). Repeat this on the remaining three sides so that all lines are consistent. The boxes can be any size, depending on how tight you would like your spirals to be (Fig 5.55).

3 Make a vertical stab cut along each of the diagonal lines on all four sides. A stab cut on a concave spiral forms the section that will become the hollow.

4 Begin to form the hollow section (Fig 5.56). Place your chisel about ⅛in (3mm) away from the stab cut on one side of the diagonal line at a 45° angle, and push the chisel towards the stab cut to remove the wood. Repeat this along the diagonals on all sides.

6 Having formed one side of the V section, you need to remove wood from the other side of the stab cut to complete the V (Fig 5.57). This is executed in the same way as before (Fig 5.58).

7 To deepen the V shape, take a round rasp file and push it back and forth along the diagonal hollows on all four sides (Fig 5.59). Keep the momentum going along the length of wood until the hollow is formed. Note that the shape of the V has evolved into a U (or fluted) shape (Fig 5.60). When each V is sufficiently hollowed, each flute should merge and form a peak between.

8 Continue shaping even when the two stems separate as you reach the connecting sections at the top of the barley twist.

9 Using a flat rasp file, round the corner edges so that the peaked sections follow the shape of the hollowed sections. You may have to do a bit more work with the rounded rasp file to deepen the hollow a bit more where the corners have been removed, as well as 'tweak' the entry and exit points at the top and bottom of the spiral (Fig 5.60).

10 Your completed spirals should be evenly spaced and smooth (Fig 5.61).

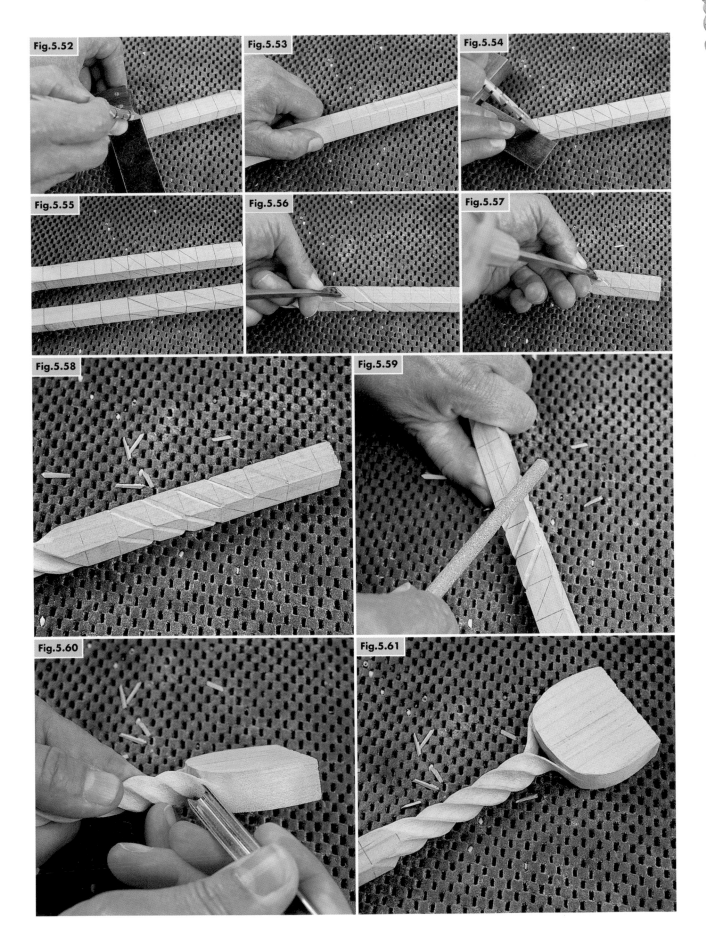

Fig.5.52

Fig.5.53

Fig.5.54

Fig.5.55

Fig.5.56

Fig.5.57

Fig.5.58

Fig.5.59

Fig.5.60

Fig.5.61

FINISHING TECHNIQUES

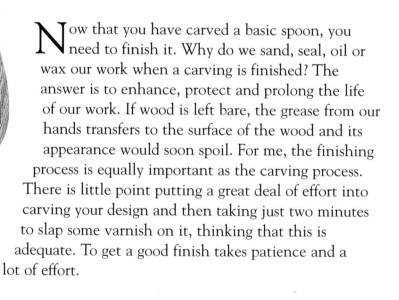

Now that you have carved a basic spoon, you need to finish it. Why do we sand, seal, oil or wax our work when a carving is finished? The answer is to enhance, protect and prolong the life of our work. If wood is left bare, the grease from our hands transfers to the surface of the wood and its appearance would soon spoil. For me, the finishing process is equally important as the carving process. There is little point putting a great deal of effort into carving your design and then taking just two minutes to slap some varnish on it, thinking that this is adequate. To get a good finish takes patience and a lot of effort.

I like my work to be very tactile. A piece of work finished well feels warm and sensual to the touch. I like my work to be sanded to a smooth, silky finish, although I appreciate that not everyone feels the same. If I have the opportunity I watch (or listen to) TV while sanding away – that way the 'fed up with sanding' syndrome doesn't kick in as soon as it might otherwise. Some people actually sand the different sections as they go along to save the work at the end. If you don't like to sand your work, you will have to ensure your work is pleasing to the eye by learning to carve perfectly clean and even cuts.

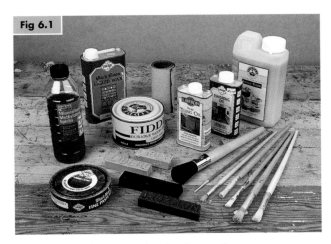

All the materials you need to finish your lovespoons, including sandpaper, sanding sealer or shellac, wax, finishing oil and brushes.

SANDPAPERS

Sandpaper comes in different grades or 'grit', and works by wearing away wood rather than tearing fibres. Sandpaper is composed of backing paper – cloth, fibre, paper or web – to which grain is firmly glued. It is the relative coarseness of the grain that removes wood at different rates. A lower number, e.g. 80, indicates a coarse grit with fast wood removal and a higher number, e.g. 600, indicates a fine grit with a smooth finish.

There are a number of different types of sandpapers, including Garnet Paper, Aluminium Oxide, Silicon Carbide and

Wet and Dry. The most commonly available, which is ideal for wood, is white aluminium oxide paper.

Sandpaper can be bought in sheet form relatively cheaply or in lengths. I particularly like VSM's Vitex, a cloth-backed sandpaper which is available in lengths from specialist stores. It is quite expensive, but lasts much longer than other alternatives.

Some people like to start sanding with 120 or 150 grit, but I prefer 180 or 240 grit. Sand along the grain rather than across it – scratch marks are less noticeable that way and much easier to remove. When I have done as much as I can with the first grade of sandpaper, I substitute for a higher grade, e.g. 320, then 400 and finally, 600, making sure that there are no scratches on the surface and that the whole area feels smooth.

Once sanding is complete, you need to contemplate the best product to finish your work. There are two main choices: a shellac finish that coats and protects the wood, or an oil finish that penetrates and protects the wood. I have not included a section on stains as I think a natural wood finish is more pleasing for lovespoon carving.

Note: Please take care when using any of the following products. They are toxic, flammable and can be dangerous if not used properly, so use in a well-ventilated room, replace caps or lids once finished, keep out of children's reach at all times, keep away from heat and flames and above all, do not ingest.

SANDING SEALER (OR SHELLAC)

The purified form of shellac comes from the scales of the female lac insect. These are collected and mixed with alcohol and other concoctions to make a solution. It forms the basis of French polishing.

Shellac is available as pure shellac flakes, button polish, sanding sealer or shellac polish/shellac sealer. I particularly like Fiddes' shellac polish which has a satin finish and does not become glossy like other brands of sealer or varnish.

Shellac should only be applied after sanding has been thoroughly carried out. It seals the wood to give a protective surface and can be used on bare wood before wax is applied or after oiling, but it is not waterproof and therefore unsuitable for outdoors.

Before applying shellac (see Fig 6.2), shake the bottle well as the properties separate when left for any length of time – a white creamy substance settles at the bottom and a pale golden liquid sits on top. Applied to wood, it dries quickly, replacing the air in the pores of the timber. As it dries, the grain is lifted and, as a result, the wood feels coarse, which means it requires further sanding, but only do this once the sealer is completely dry. Brush away any white powder before applying a second coat of shellac. Let this dry – overnight if you can – then, using a very fine sandpaper, lightly sand down once more (use glass or flour paper if you can get hold of it or, alternatively, 3M's

Fig 6.2

Applying a coat of shellac seals the surface of the spoon.

Tri-M-ite Frecut). Again, remove any white powder before applying a couple of coats of wax. Clean your brush with methylated spirits and wash with washing-up liquid and water.

OILS

There are a number of oil finishes on the market that you can choose from and each one has a specific usage. Oils penetrate and soak into the wood and may take 24 hours or more to dry. They do not raise the grain like shellac, so there is no need for sanding between coats.

FINISHING OIL

This is a blend of high quality oils that, once applied, provide a smooth, soft sheen and enhances the natural colour of the wood. It is resistant to heat, water, alcohol and food acids. It is suitable for surfaces such as kitchen or bathroom units, garden and indoor furniture, turned work and children's toys.

Apply a thin coat to clean wood using a brush or cloth. Allow to penetrate into the wood for approximately ten minutes, wiping off any excess with a clean cloth before the oil dries or becomes sticky. Allow to dry before applying further coats.

TUNG OIL

Tung oil is pressed from the tung nut and is a natural, penetrating, nontoxic oil. It is hard-wearing, dries naturally (no driers added) and is one of the most resilient oil finishes on the market. It can be used on objects that come in contact with food, on toys, kitchen worktops, utensils and interior woodwork.

For ease of application, the first few coats of tung oil should be diluted with white spirit (up to 50%). Apply a coat onto clean wood using a brush or cloth and allow to penetrate for approximately 15 minutes before wiping off excess with a clean cloth. Failure to wipe off any excess will prevent further coats penetrating and will also leave a sticky surface.

Allow up to four days for the oil to dry before applying further coats. The final coat should be applied using pure undiluted tung oil. Again, wipe off excess after 15 minutes. Apply a few coats of wax after the oil has dried to give a satin sheen to your work.

DANISH OIL

Danish oil is made up of a special blend of oil, resins, driers and solvents. It is based on tung oil and is very easy to apply. It gives a natural low-lustre finish to all timbers, and is suitable for all interior and exterior woodwork. It is hard and durable and can also be painted over or waxed.

Apply a thin coat onto clean wood using a brush or cloth. Allow to penetrate into the wood for approximately ten minutes, wiping off any excess with a clean cloth before the oil dries or becomes sticky. Allow to dry before applying further coats.

WAXES

Wax is designed to bring out the natural beauty of wood. It protects, nourishes and provides a lasting sheen on all wood products. It can be used on all types of timbers – old or new – and comes in different forms. It can be applied directly to wood or over shellac and oil finishes. Beeswax, carnuba wax and paraffin wax are available in pure blocks, creamy pastes or liquids – the last two are made from a blend of waxes.

The three main waxes I use are Fiddes' Supreme Polish, Liberon Black Bison Fine Paste Wax and Liberon Black Bison Liquid Wax. All provide a good finish and are durable. I use whichever I think will serve me best for the job. If I have a lot of detail, I use the liquid wax as it's much easier to apply and take off (see Fig 6.3). If something requires waxing, I usually apply two or three coats. The first dries for approximately an hour and I then buff it off. I leave the second or third coat overnight before polishing off, and this helps to give a deep, lasting sheen. The wax can be taken off using a brush, an old cloth (I prefer a towel as the loops aid removal), wire wool or a web-fibre pad. Brushes used for liquid wax can be cleaned with white spirit. There are three different waxes available:

BEESWAX

Available in blocks of 100% pure wax and is used to make wax polishes. It needs to be dissolved in pure turpentine to make it soft enough to apply.

CARNUBA WAX

This is a hard vegetable wax and gives a hard-wearing finish. It is too brittle to use on its own, so if you want to try it, it should ideally be mixed with other waxes.

PARAFFIN WAX

This white wax can be melted to seal the end grain of timber or mixed with other waxes to make a home-made polish. Paraffin wax gives a nice, clear finish.

Fig 6.3

Finishing the completed spoon with liquid wax.

SHARPENING TECHNIQUES

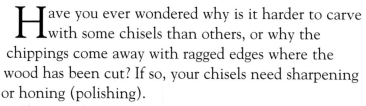

Have you ever wondered why is it harder to carve with some chisels than others, or why the chippings come away with ragged edges where the wood has been cut? If so, your chisels need sharpening or honing (polishing).

Sharp tools are essential for good work. Learning sharpening techniques takes time, but it is time well spent as blunt chisels or chisels sharpened with wrong bevels all make for poor cuts and hard work. Don't expect to be an expert within two minutes – give yourself time to learn and try to practise as much as you can (on old chisels if possible).

As a beginner to carving, we are only too pleased to pick up a chisel and work with it, unaware that as we work the chisel loses its edge until it is too difficult to work with. This is because the tool becomes blunt and we have to use more effort to remove wood. At this point, accidents are more likely to happen. Be warned: I know friends who have needed microsurgery for cuts caused by blunt chisels. They may be blunt on wood, but they're still sharp enough to cause a major injury.

Learn how to recognize a blunt chisel. It took me a while before I could see the white edge that everyone kept referring to when they told me a chisel was blunt. Eventually, by turning the blade to face me and moving it in different directions, I finally caught the light along the blade edge. Try it and you should see small, white specks or a continuous white line along the blade, depending on its bluntness (see Figs 7.1 and 7.2). Another telltale sign is if you have to push the chisel through the wood with more pressure, or if you cut the wood and notice small, rough sections where the chisel has gone through. If this is the case, the blunt section has actually torn the wood rather than cut through the fibres.

You may be able to call on the services of a friend or partner to sharpen your chisels as I have, but this is not the long-term answer. In short, you must learn to sharpen yourself. It's not easy, but nothing worth learning is. Learning to sharpen takes time and patience, but it comes with practice and ultimately saves you time to spend on carving.

To cover this subject in detail would fill an entire book of its own. We strongly recommend reading Chris Pye's *Woodcarving Tools, Materials and Equipment* for in-depth information on sharpening and how to modify tools, and Dick Onians' *Essential Woodcarving Techniques* which also provides detailed information on sharpening (see page 133 for further details).

In order to begin, you need to have a sharpening stone and some lubrication to wash away the swarf (metal particles). There are so many different stones available on the market, which one should you pick? There are: oil stones, ceramic stones, diamond stones, Arkansas stones, slip stones, grinding wheels, rubberized wheels, whet wheels, felt wheels, floppy dollies – to name but a few.

Fig 7.1

Fig 7.2

In the following section, we outline the least expensive way of sharpening first, using wet and dry sandpaper, and then look at more convenient methods, such as the rubberized wheel and whet wheel. The preference is yours, of course, and while I would recommend that you buy one of the latter at a later stage, you may want to start with wet and dry sandpaper first.

WET AND DRY SANDPAPER

I was first shown this method at a British Woodcarvers' Association symposium. As a carver with just a few years' experience, I was beginning to learn how to sharpen and found this method invaluable. It is a slow method, but enabled me to get the hang of it and feel less afraid of having a go, as I wasn't so worried about ruining my tools. It is also relatively inexpensive. You need wet and dry sandpaper, water, some honing compound (which lasts a very long time), a strip of leather about 6–8in (152–203mm) long, and maybe a strip of metal (such as a scraper) to go under the sandpaper to give a level surface.

METHOD

1 Place the metal strip under the sandpaper (180 or 240 grit) and, if possible, pin all edges of the sandpaper to the workbench. If there are any dips or bumps on your workbench or surface, it will cause problems when sharpening.

2 Apply water to the sandpaper. Water acts as a lubricant and washes away the tiny, metal particles ground off the chisel.

3 Take note of the bevel at the back of the blade (this is normally set at a 25–35° angle depending on the make of chisel, and is the section where the metal tapers down to become a thin edge). Once positioned on the sandpaper, the chisel needs to be ground at the same angle. To do this, position the heel first (the thick end of the bevel), then lower the blade end down. As the edge gets closer to the sandpaper, it will displace the water. When this happens you should have the correct angle (see Fig 7.3).

4 Keeping the angle of bevel consistent at all times, place the chisel at the furthest end of the sandpaper so that one edge rests on the surface and the other is raised in the air.

In a continuous movement, pull the chisel towards you, turning it as you move so that, as the chisel reaches the end of the sandpaper, the edge of the chisel – previously up in the air – now rests on the sandpaper and vice versa. Repeat this, moving the chisel back to your original starting point. Continue to move back and forth using fresh sandpaper, regularly checking for white bits along the edge of the blade. (If white spots appear in one or two places, concentrate on these areas only.) Use a slip stone to remove the burr formed on the inside bevel (see page 51).

5 At this point, even though the bevel needs to be honed, the chisel should still slice through the wood. If it doesn't, continue to repeat the process. Replace with a fresh piece of sandpaper if necessary.

6 Next, hone your chisel. Rub some compound onto the leather and move the chisel back and forth as in step 4 to smooth the marks out of the metal – not too much compound otherwise the chisel will glide over the surface rather than create friction. During the sharpening process, grit from the sandpaper cuts small grooves into the metal and it is these that need to be polished away. A way to avoid spending a lot of time polishing out the marks is to change to a higher grit sandpaper to attain a razor-sharp edge.

7 Having successfully followed the above, you should now have a chisel that is ready for action. Test it on a waste piece of wood before commencing work on your project.

ELECTRICAL SHARPENERS

There are two pieces of electrical sharpening equipment you can use: a rubberized wheel and a whet wheel. Both are extremely useful in different ways.

RUBBERIZED WHEEL

The rubber of this wheel has little silicone carbide particles implanted in it which increases its sharpening capacity.

Rubberized wheels can be purchased from specialized woodcraft outlets or direct from a manufacturer such as Ashley Iles Tools Ltd (see page 132 for suppliers). A great feature of the Ashley Iles product is that they offer both right-handed and left-handed versions. Whichever supplier you use, it is worth buying one direct as a complete kit, comprising rubberized wheel, floppy dolly, polishing compound, dressing stone and a spotlight. The advantage of this product is that the rotation of the wheel turns away from you rather than towards you. With cheaper grinders from DIY stores, you will find that the wheels rotate towards you and you will have to alter the rotation before it can be used. This is not a straightforward job – mine was bought for me and I spent a few hours breaking seals and pulling apart the components before I could reverse it. (And by doing this, you also invalidate your guarantee.)

The principle of sharpening chisels is the same, irrespective of the method – the chisel must move from one edge to the other while maintaining the same angle on the bevel. Two reasons why the Ashley Iles sharpener is unique is because the chisel is held at a 90° angle to the wheel so that the blade edge is parallel within the width of the wheel (see Fig 7.4), and secondly, the spotlight fixed to the wheel throws a shadow so that it is easier to tell when the chisel is positioned at the correct angle.

Note: do not put too much pressure on the chisel when holding it against the wheel. The reason is that the speed at which the wheel turns generates a great deal of heat within the chisel and, with too much pressure, the steel of the chisel can take on a blue hue (especially around the edges where the steel is thinnest). This is called 'losing the temper'.

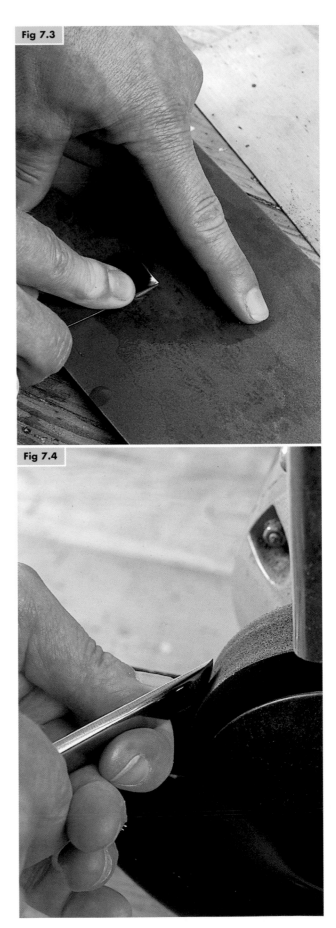

Fig 7.3

Fig 7.4

Check your chisel regularly for heat build-up and if you find this happening, try the following:

- Hold the chisel against the wheel with less pressure.

- If possible, let the chisel cool naturally.

- Keep a jar of water close by and periodically remove the chisel from the wheel and dip it in the jar to cool it down. By doing this you are cooling the steel, and adding to the longevity of your chisel.

Once sharpening is complete, hone your chisel on the cloth dolly (see Fig 7.5). First place a small amount of honing paste onto the wheel and position your chisel on top of this. I use green compound but there are other colours: each one indicating a different grade of paste for polishing.

This time place the chisel horizontally on the cloth dolly wheel. If placed vertically at the 90° angle – as on the rubberized wheel – the corner of the chisel is likely to catch in the wheel as it rotates, snatching it out of your hand and causing untold damage. Gently rock your chisel back and forth to hone the whole edge, making sure that you remove all scratches. Having polished the outside bevel, turn the chisel over and polish the inside to remove the burr that will have formed during the sharpening process.

Once correctly sharpened, the chisel should glide through the wood without visible trace of damage to the fibres. A sure sign of a well-sharpened tool is if the chip curls into itself as the chisel removes it from the wood.

WHET WHEEL

I have only recently purchased a Tormek whet wheel and I am quite taken with it. You don't have to worry about the possibility of heat build-up in the steel because water is continually carried over the surface keeping the steel cool. Whetstones run at a slower speed than bench grinders, enabling better tool control. There is no front or back to this machine so you have the choice of whether you grind with the edge (where the wheel rotates away from you, i.e. if you are sharpening freehand, without jigs) or against the edge (where the wheel rotates towards you). If using this latter method, I recommend you use jigs (which are supplied separately) otherwise the tool is likely to dig into the stone.

Fig 7.5

My whet wheel has a 'Super Grindstone': a man-made ceramic stone containing grains of aluminium-oxide which gives a sharp edge to your tools. It also has many jigs and a 'Stone Grader' (available separately). This feature transforms the stone from a fast grinder to a fine grinder with the same sharpening abilities. It also restores the stone to its original condition, removing any glaze and dust that may make the wheel ineffective. The fine side of the Stone Grader gives a very fine finish to your tools and is excellent for lighter grindings such as those on woodcarving tools and smaller knives. It also has a leather honing wheel and is supplied with honing compound.

Unlike rubberized wheel grinders, chisels on the whet wheel are positioned with their edges held horizontal on the stone and are rocked from left to right to sharpen along the edge. There are a few disadvantages, as follows:

- When using fishtail chisels. When I tilt the tool from one corner to the other, it is difficult to see if the edge of the tool is touching the stone or not, which means I don't know if I am sharpening the corner too much, rounding it off instead or not sharpening it enough.

- The wheels can be softer and wear out more quickly.

- Due to the slower speed of the 1200 machine, the honing wheel is ineffective for polishing the bevel unless you spend a long time at the machine. To be fair, the handbook advises that 'usually you do not need to hone the surface at all after grinding on a wet grindstone. You just remove the burr, which remains after the grinding'. However, as I like a polished bevel, it does mean that I need another machine so that I can polish my tools once I have completed the sharpening.

SHARPENING AIDS

SLIP STONES
One final aspect to sharpening chisels is removing the burr from the inside edge of the chisel. A burr is what is formed along the edge of the blade where the steel has been ground away. It doesn't always break off and so has to be actively removed. This can be done either by using the edge of the honing wheel of your grinder or with a slip stone.

Slip stones come in various shapes and can be used to suit most chisels. They are held at an angle to the inside edge of the chisel and moved back and forth across the edge until the burr is removed. It is possible to give the inside bevel an uneven edge – a fluted effect – if you use the slip stone in one place for too long. To overcome this, hold the chisel in your left hand, position the slip stone in your right hand at the corner furthest away from you, and pull it in one fluid, forwards movement until it reaches the corner nearest to you.

To check the burr is removed, run your nail from the shank of the chisel outwards and over the edge. If your nail glides easily over the surface without the slightest bump, then you can assume the burr has been removed. If your nail feels as though it stops in its tracks (however slight the bump) there is still some metal to remove and you must continue working the slip stone.

LEATHER STROP
Another essential sharpening aid for the workshop, a leather strop is a piece of wood to which a strip of leather is adhered. Used in conjunction with honing compound, it is very effective for sharpening chisels. They should ideally be stropped every ten minutes to keep all your tools in good order, so keep one by your side as you work (see also Equipment and Helpful Aids, page 12).

Patterns

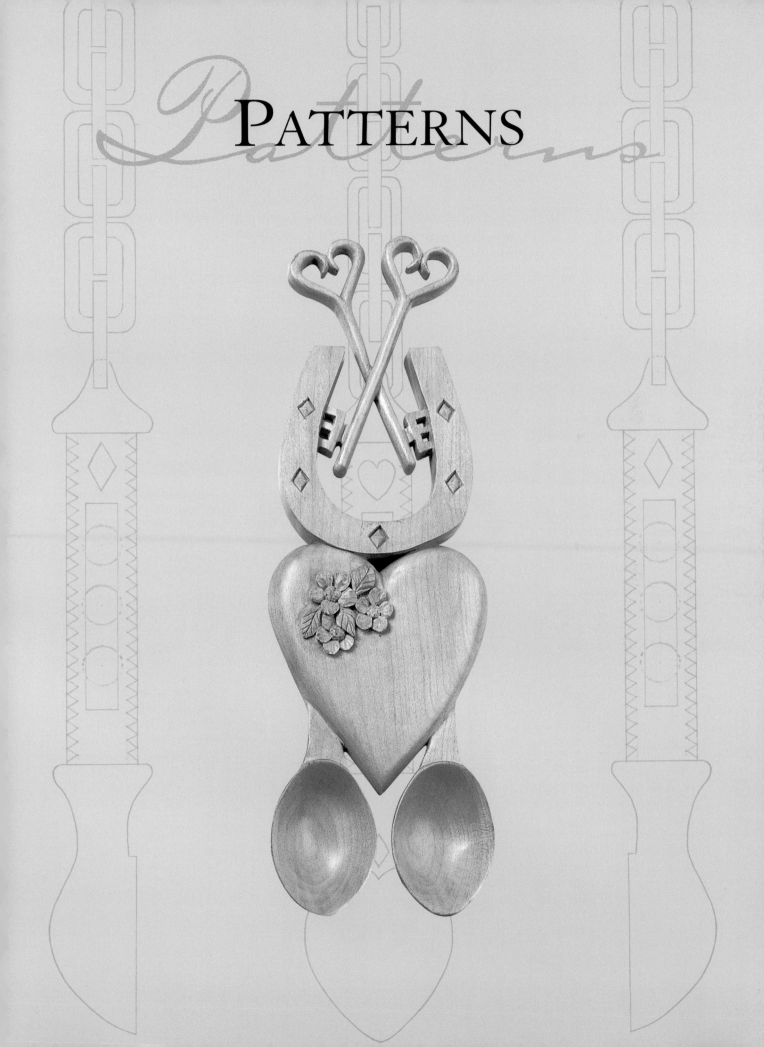

RAM'S HORN SPOON

This spoon was designed for someone whose star sign is Aries – a person with many interests and an ability to turn their hand to many things. These elements have been incorporated into the spoon's design. The design is less traditional than other patterns, but still retains the custom of telling a story.

I'm not sure of the origin of Jesmo (John Crow). There are advantages to this wood – it is inexpensive, and contains many attractive shades of orange. But it is a heavy, difficult wood, and in places the grain is short which increases the possibility of breakage. Its open cell structure leaves small, light dots when carved, too. Worst of all, though, is the putrid smell it generates when cut on the scroll saw.

The tips of the horns are designed to be high points sweeping down in a flowing movement and then up again as they reach the ram's head. The section from the brow to the nose is level with the tip of the horns with each side of the head slanting downwards to form the head. Viewed as a cross section, it looks like an inverted V. The nose to the bottom jaw also slants down towards the tentacles without resting on them, thus creating a three-faceted effect.

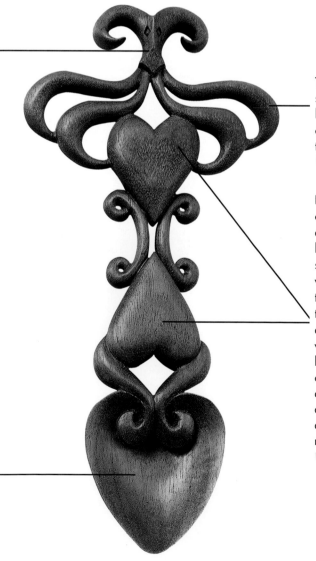

The four tentacles have been stepped down from the jaw line and rounded to complement the shape of the head.

Both hearts have been cushioned and the connecting arms joining them reduced lower than the hearts to separate them, and offer variation in the levels. These too have been rounded. As the length of the connecting arm forms a circle, slope the wood downwards so that it is lower at the point where the circle connects back to the arm (as if going under the top arm). The shapes in the design give a sense of movement and rhythm.

To shape the bowl, stab cut around the swirls and remove waste wood to form the internal bowl shape. Once complete, shape the swirls so that they remain raised but resting on the bowl, and the bowl appears to form its natural shape at the base of the swirls. Once satisfied, slightly round the edges.

SIZE

10 x 4in (254 x 102mm)

TYPE OF WOOD

Jesmo (John Crow)

SYMBOLS AND MEANINGS

The ram's horns refer to the sign of Aries, sometimes referred to as the glyph.

The octopus-like tentacles emanating from the horns indicate an involvement in many things in life.

The hearts show love. The twists and turns in the bowl that connect the hearts together show an active person.

WEDDING SPOON

This spoon was originally intended as a wedding present and the design for the hexagons was to include meaningful mementos for the couple. Sadly, the wedding was called off, so these were modified slightly to create a generic wedding spoon instead. For your spoon, introduce your own personalized elements. This design will suit the more experienced carver.

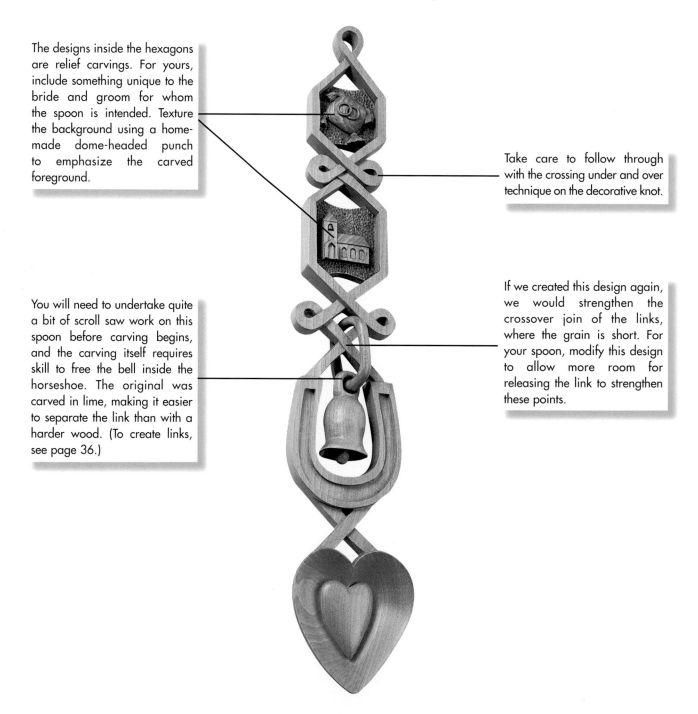

The designs inside the hexagons are relief carvings. For yours, include something unique to the bride and groom for whom the spoon is intended. Texture the background using a home-made dome-headed punch to emphasize the carved foreground.

Take care to follow through with the crossing under and over technique on the decorative knot.

You will need to undertake quite a bit of scroll saw work on this spoon before carving begins, and the carving itself requires skill to free the bell inside the horseshoe. The original was carved in lime, making it easier to separate the link than with a harder wood. (To create links, see page 36.)

If we created this design again, we would strengthen the crossover join of the links, where the grain is short. For your spoon, modify this design to allow more room for releasing the link to strengthen these points.

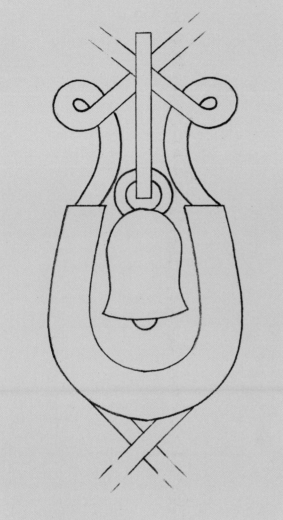

Alternative design avoiding the weak crossover point.

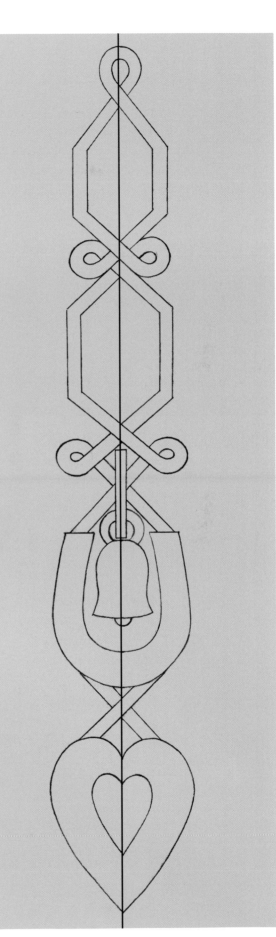

SIZE
17 x 2in (432 x 51mm)

TYPE OF WOOD
Lime

SYMBOLS AND MEANINGS
The wedding rings represent the union of a couple before God.

The church symbolizes marriage and faith.

The horseshoe is a token of good luck.

The bell represents the church bells proclaiming the couple's commitment.

The heart expresses love.

The heart-shaped bowl expresses a wish for a full and bountiful life.

CORNER MOTIF SPOON

This design is based on a motif originally intended to form a design for a border pattern in this book. On showing the design to a friend, she said it would be a good pattern for a spoon, so I added a bowl. I have to say she was right.

The top of the spoon is influenced by various cupolas found on churches and mosques. Inside the cupola, I carved the initials of myself and Clive as authors of this book. Clive's initials are shown as a reversed C with a G and my initials are shown as an S, symbolized by a swan, with the L continuing from the front curve of the swan's breast to create the webbed foot. These interlocking initials are raised and the sunken background has been textured for added effect.

Use the cupola to carve your own initials, a cushioned heart, a horseshoe – or whatever you like. Look at the symbol templates on page 120, select a motif and transfer it to your design.

For the central part of the spoon, intertwine the strands using a crossing under and over effect (as in a Celtic knot design). Twist each side to create a camber effect, changing direction of the camber as the curve changes course.

The crossover point as it joins the bowl is quite fragile, so be careful not to put too much pressure on the spoon while carving.

Our spoon was carved in English walnut. It has a rich tone of colour which will be much admired once you have sealed and waxed the wood. I like using walnut – it can be a bit hard, but it carves nicely and holds a great deal of detail, although the detail is less clear on the darker areas of the wood.

SIZE
12 x 3in (305 x 76mm)

TYPE OF WOOD
Walnut

SYMBOLS AND MEANINGS
Celtic knots represent everlasting love.

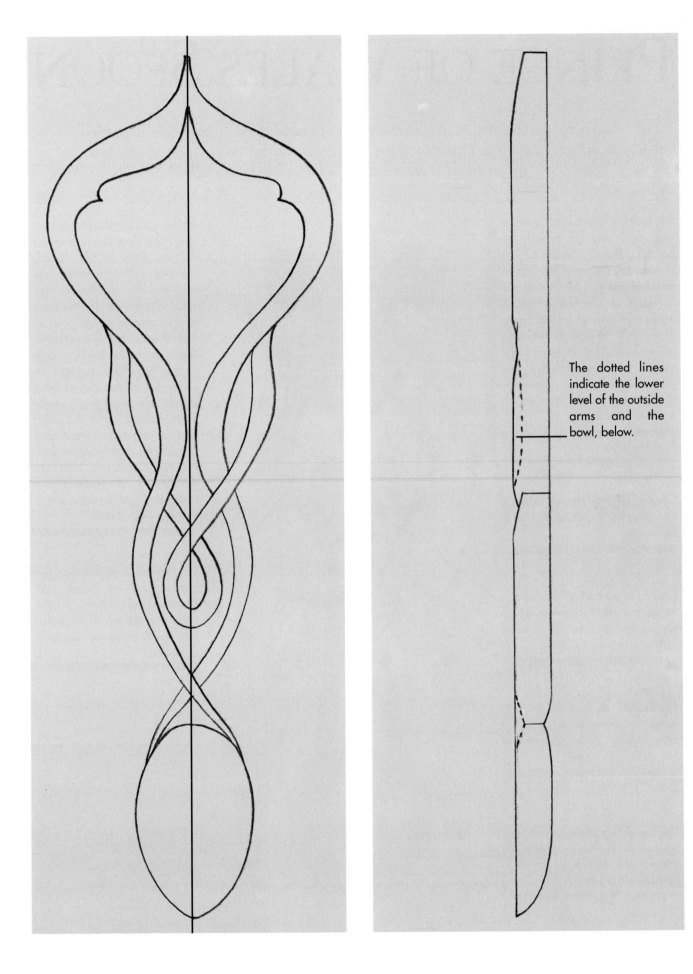

The dotted lines indicate the lower level of the outside arms and the bowl, below.

VICTORIA'S SPOON

This spoon was designed as a christening present for Clive's great-niece, Victoria. A hand-carved spoon is a lovely, unique gift for a child. Carved in lime, it was finished with sanding sealer and wax.

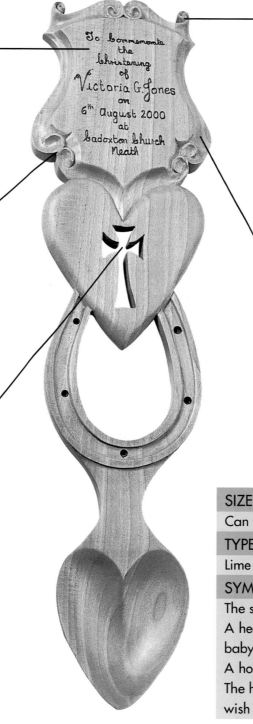

Burn the baby's name, date of birth and the name of the church onto the shield.

Approach the decorative swirls with care and patience. Make stab cuts around each one and don't exert too much pressure to avoid unsightly cut marks. To carve the swirls, choose chisels that fit the shapes – probably Nos. 7, 8, 9 or 11 with varying widths of blade. Try to carve the frame as a continual, flowing line – especially around the swirls. If you sand this area afterwards, be careful not to soften the definition of the ridge between the shaped edge and flat surface.

Fret out the cross on a scroll saw. Carve a groove in the horseshoe and drill out holes for the nails to go through.

The scroll at the back has been chamfered down to give the appearance that it is following the bend. Hollow the area inside the curl with a scalpel or a craft knife. Curl a sheet of paper to help you visualize how it should look.

When this shield was carved, the outer ¼in (6mm) or so was shaped to form a frame with a No. 8/7 or 8/10 gouge. With your spoon, hold the gouge so that it enters the wood from the outer edge of the shield at an angle of about 45°. As you move your chisel through the wood, this cut keeps the inside edge as a high point and reduces at the outer edge by about ⅛–¼in (3–6mm). Using a gouge with a deep curve adds a concave effect to your frame and enhances the overall appearance of the shield.

SIZE

Can vary

TYPE OF WOOD

Lime

SYMBOLS AND MEANINGS

The shield symbolizes protection. A heart shows love for the newborn baby, and the cross symbolizes faith. A horseshoe signifies good luck. The heart-shaped bowl expresses a wish for a full and bountiful life.

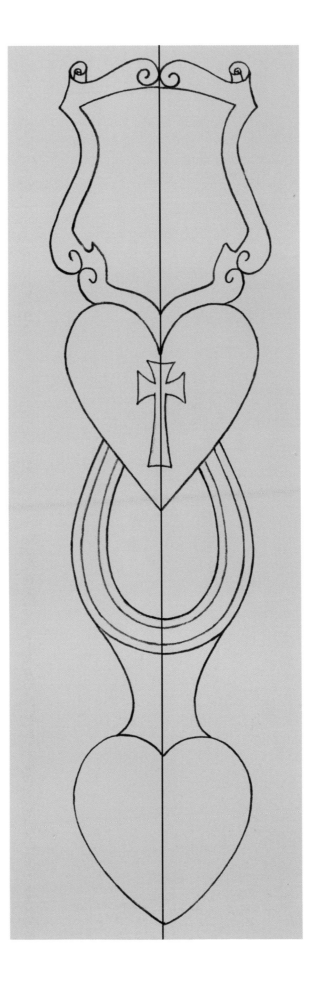

BIRTHDAY SPOON

The design for this spoon was at the request of a friend for a birthday present. It has been carved in elm which complements the design – especially on the right-hand side of the daffodil where the grain follows the contour of the leaves.

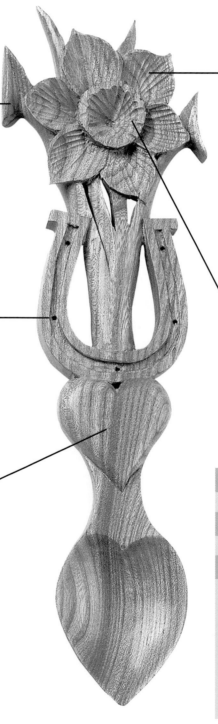

Carve the leaves to appear behind the daffodil. Remove the wood and shape the leaves. For added realism, bend some of them by sloping the leaf on one side. As it joins the fold in the leaf, slope the bent side to form a valley. To help you visualize the effect, take a V tool and some waste wood and carve a groove into it – this is how it should look.

Carve the horseshoe with or without a channel. If you carve one, make sure that you keep the edges straight as you remove the wood – by no means should you undercut them. Stab cut along the lines first before removing the waste wood.

Carve the heart to create a cushioned effect. To do this, round the edges, then reduce unnecessary wood on the area between the heart and the bowl to make the heart stand out.

Six petals surround the trumpet – three on top, three below. The outer tip of the petal forms a high point. Stab cut around the petals to gradually remove the wood, going deeper towards the trumpet, but do not undercut the trumpet at this stage – leave it as a solid block until the end. Remove the wood inside the flower petals to a good depth – the deeper the petal base, the more the trumpet will stand out.

For the trumpet, leave about ⅛in (3mm) around the circumference to create the 'frilly' edge. Remove the waste wood from the centre so that the outer edge of the flower tapers in towards the base of the trumpet. Once satisfied that the shape is right, undercut the trumpet and tidy it up. Finally, with a No. 8/3 or 11/3 gouge, carve grooves inside the trumpet and work the frilly effect around the rim. Carve some on the petals, too, if desired.

SIZE
12 x 3in (305 x 76mm)

TYPE OF WOOD
Elm

SYMBOLS AND MEANINGS
A daffodil represents affection, but is also the national emblem of Wales – the recipient's home. The horseshoe signifies good luck. The heart indicates love, and the heart-shaped bowl signifies a wish for a full and bountiful life.

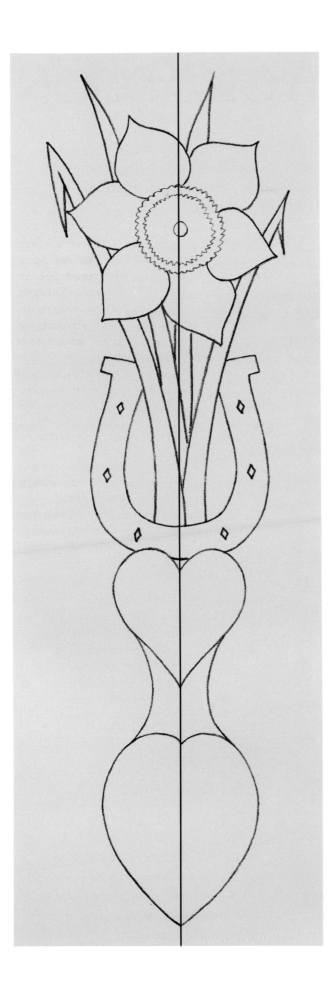

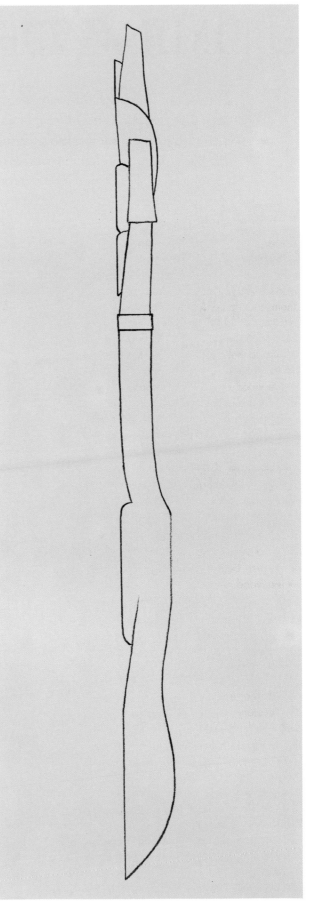

COMING OF AGE SPOON

This spoon was carved for a young man as a gift for his 18th birthday. A very active person, he is involved in canoeing, rock climbing and snorkelling and, at the time, studying English at university, too, so I incorporated some of these elements to produce an unusual design.

Taper the figure 18 at the end of the canoe by making the outer edges of the figures high points and evenly reducing the wood inwards towards the outer edges of the end of the canoe. At the crossover point of the figure 8, stab cut each side of the line, and reduce the wood to create the crossing over and under effect.

Shape the oars. Round these off until they meet the paddles and keep that section flat. Once satisfied with the overall shape, undercut the oars to give them a rounded appearance. In cast light, this creates a nice shadow.

Stab cut around the oars and reduce the wood around these by about ⅛in (2–3mm). Leave the arms of the oars square at this stage while you work on the canoe, and round them off later.

Hollow out the bowl, remembering to maintain the shape of the front tip of the canoe as you work.

If you wish, use the oars lain across the top of the canoe to contain information such as the date of the birthday – as I have – by burning in the details with a pyrography machine.

The spoon is shaped as a canoe, and I used the front of the canoe to help form the bowl into a heart shape. Curve the canoe on both sides, working from the centre to the outer edges. Maintain the slope of the curve of the canoe under the oars. Stab cut the centre oval which forms the seat. Remove waste wood from the oval section before transferring your design, then carve the relief pattern.

SIZE
Can vary

TYPE OF WOOD
Elm

SYMBOLS AND MEANINGS
The canoe and rock climber represent an interest in outdoor pursuits.
The figure 18 represents 'coming of age'.
The heart-shaped bowl expresses a wish for a bountiful life.

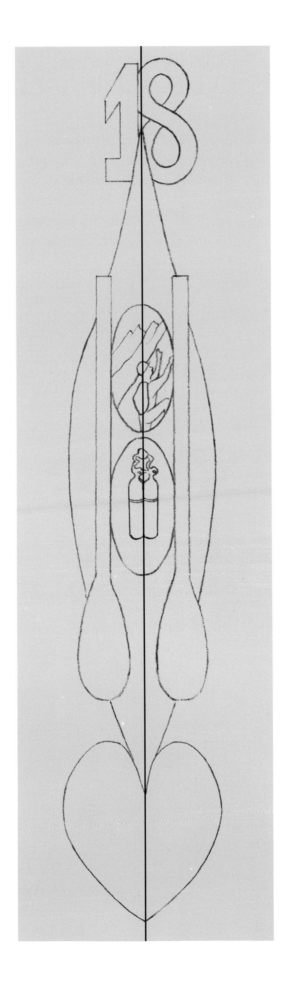

LOVEBIRDS SPOON

Clive created this spoon which he adapted from the design for a basic lovespoon (see page 26). He has carved similar designs a few times, changing the oval feature on each occasion.

Clive is partial to carving lovebirds. For him, they reinforce the romantic origins of lovespoons to court a girl – a custom which has gone out of fashion.

Carve the horseshoe with a groove running through the centre. To do this, make vertical stab cuts along the inner lines and remove the waste wood. Try to maintain straight edges – if your stab cut is angled in any way it will cause you problems, especially towards the outer edge. Since this spoon was carved, we have been advised that there are traditionally seven nail holes inside a horseshoe rather than six, so you may wish to add one more.

This design was slightly modified as it was carved. Take a look at where the tails of the birds and the horseshoe meet. On the finished spoon, the tails hang over the outer edge of the horseshoe. Because the grain is short at this point, the tails are susceptible to breakage. To overcome this, the pattern has been altered so that the outer lugs of the horseshoe face outwards with the tail resting on them, which makes the weak point stronger.

Round the hearts for a full-cushioned effect.

The oval feature is extremely versatile and can be used to display different symbols. Remove the waste wood from the background of the oval to allow the shape of the daffodil to stand proud.

Chip-carve the outside edge of the oval, and texture the area between this and the daffodil using a nail punch. For further details on creating triangular recesses, see page 25.

SIZE
12 x 3in (305 x 76mm)

TYPE OF WOOD
Lime

SYMBOLS AND MEANINGS
The lovebirds represent a couple deeply in love.
A horseshoe signifies good luck.
Double hearts indicate a reciprocal love. Also, that 'we two are one', or to ask 'love me as I love you'.
A flower expresses affection, but the daffodil is also the national emblem of Wales where the couple live.
The heart-shaped bowl signifies a wish for a full and happy life together.

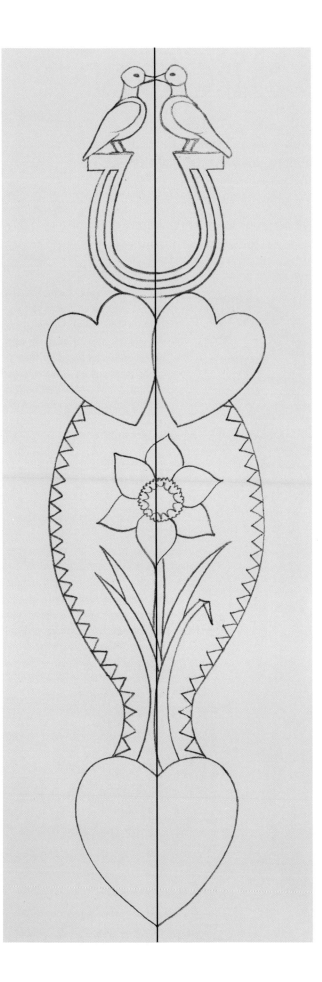

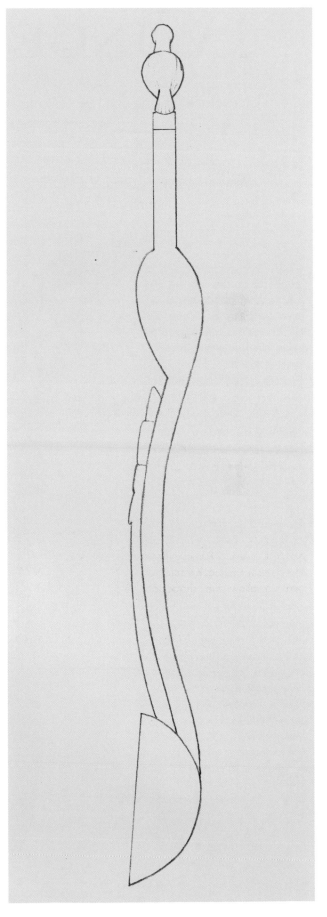

WINGED SPOON

I developed this design one evening while doodling as I talked on the phone to a good friend. I was looking for a more modern design that might appeal to younger people and be a suitable gift for an 18th or 21st birthday.

One thing I've noticed is that the top half of the Celtic knot resembles a Mickey Mouse face – I think it's the two circles at the top which give the impression of ears!

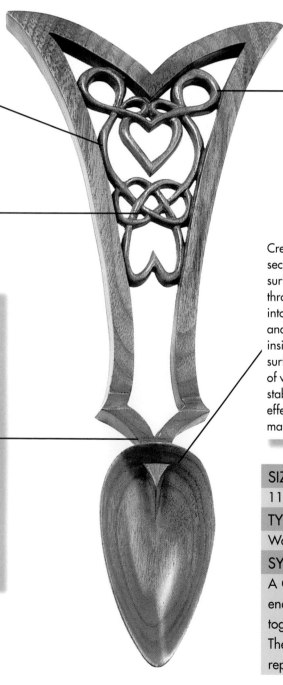

Round the edges of the Celtic knot rather than leave them flat. Be aware that the smaller areas mean that it is more awkward to clean and sand.

Walnut is quite strong and copes with the intricate, but delicate crossover sections inside the Celtic knot.

The base of the frame, where it meets at a point, has been carved to look as if it 'pierces' through the bowl of the spoon. To achieve this effect, reduce/lower wood from the area above the bowl, likewise taking the same amount from the frame area on the inside of the bowl. As you do this, maintain the curve of the bowl. Once you are satisfied that both sides of the bowl are the same level, slightly undercut each side of the point where it rests on the bowl. Take care as you work the area to maintain the 'flow' of the curve of the bowl.

Reduce the knot so that it sits below the outer frame of the spoon. With any Celtic knot, make sure you mark high and low points to avoid one thread going over when it should go under. If you are interrupted during carving, pay attention to what you were doing beforehand so you can continue – it is at times like these that mistakes are made.

Create a hollow effect between the bowl section and the arrow head (or top surface of the point) where it pierces through the bowl. To do this, stab cut into the wood at a slight angle across and slightly beyond the width of the inside area of the bowl. Keeping the surface of the arrow flat, remove a sliver of wood from the bowl side of where the stab cut was made to give an undercut effect. It is surprising the difference this makes when light is cast upon it.

SIZE
11¾ x 5in (298 x 127mm)

TYPE OF WOOD
Walnut

SYMBOLS AND MEANINGS
A Celtic knot represents never-ending love and a wish to be together forever.
The two hearts inside the knot represent love.

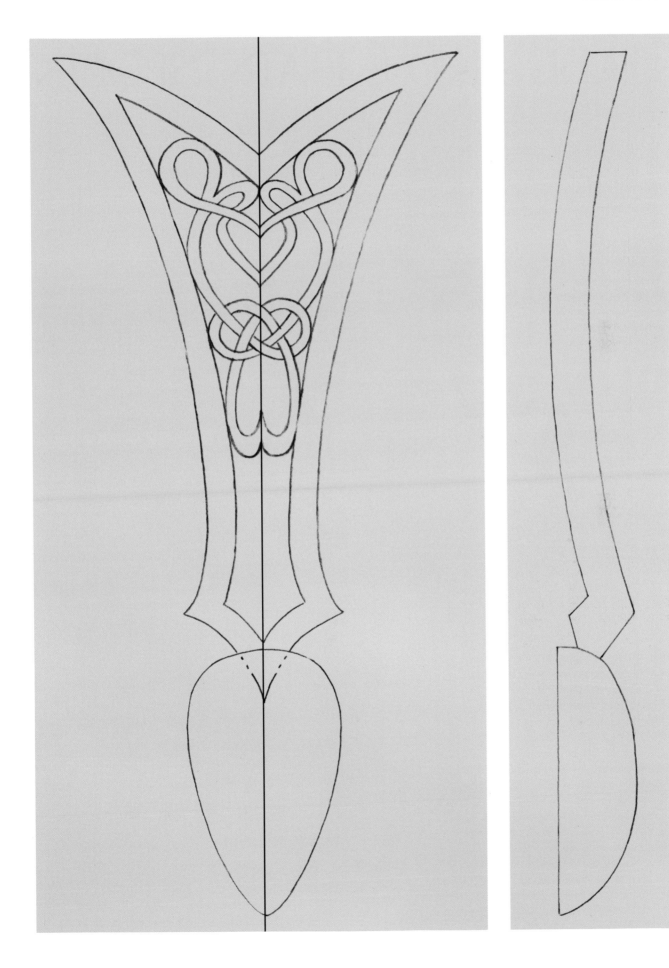

BALL AND CHAIN SPOON

Clive designed this spoon specifically for the book. When we were deciding which patterns to include, we realized that we had both a spoon with balls in a cage and a spoon with chains, but no design that featured both, so he created this combination spoon.

The spoon has been carved in lime which makes separating chains and forming balls easy. It also enhances the detail in the chip carving.

For guidance on working the chains, follow the method (see page 36).

For more details on creating balls in a cage, follow the method (see page 32).

The diamond above the heart-shaped bowl is executed in a different way. Mark the outline of the diamond with stab cuts, keeping your chisel vertical so that your edges are perfectly straight. Using a small, straight-edged chisel or a knife held at a 45° angle, remove wood from the centre point towards the outer edge. Repeat this on all four sides. Your resulting shape should look like a pyramid: the centre peak level with the surface of the surrounding area and each of the four sides reduced to approximately ⅟₁₆–⅛in (2mm) below the surface area. Practise this on a piece of waste wood first before attempting to carve it on your spoon.

Before cutting out the fretted hearts and diamonds, first draw the hearts on the top surface of the front profile, then drill a small hole inside the area to be removed. Use a scroll saw or fret saw to remove the internal area of the heart. Once complete, soften the square edges with a gouge, sandpaper, riffler or needle file. To make the diamond on the side, turn the spoon sideways and repeat the above method. For more on cutting a side profile on an uneven surface, see page 27.

To create triangular recesses along each pillar, see page 25.

SIZE
17¾ x 2¼in (451 x 57mm)

TYPE OF WOOD
Lime

SYMBOLS AND MEANINGS
A chain demonstrates a wish to be together forever.
Balls in a cage represent the number of children in a family, or a desire for children.
The fretted hearts indicate love.
The diamonds indicate wealth – either financial or of good fortune.
The heart-shaped bowl symbolizes a wish for a full and bountiful life.

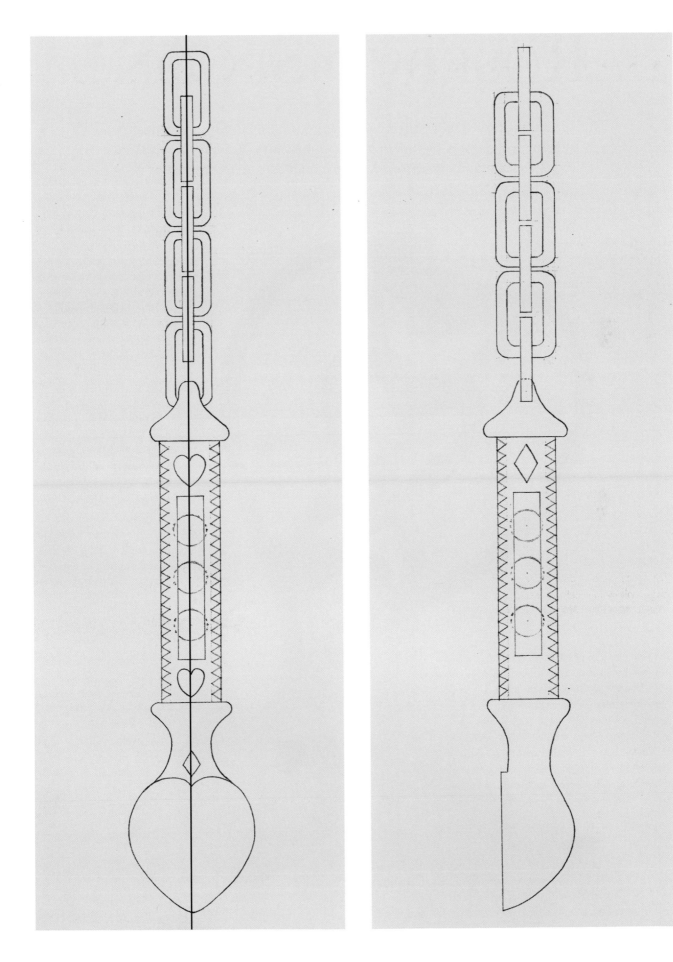

ROSEBUD SPOON

This spoon was carved as a Christmas present for a friend. She has always been encouraging and complimentary about my work, so a few years ago I designed and carved this for her to express my appreciation.

Begin the rosebuds by rounding the edges on both sides. Once done, redraw the sepals and petals onto your design. At this point, use a knife to make stab cuts around the sepals and to reduce the rosebud petals to appear as though they are cupped inside the sepal and receptacle area of the bud. As you reduce this surface, curve the petals towards the base or receptacle area so that they begin to take on a bud shape, and then do the same for the top of the bud. Make a stab cut along the edge of the petal, and reduce one side so that the top petal stands proud to create a more realistic flower. Round the outer arms of the rosebud to look like a stem. Take care as you work these fragile stems.

The brittle nature of mahogany means that it is not the easiest wood to work. Before I gave the spoon, someone borrowed it to copy the design, and while in her care it was subject to an accident. Such is life! As a result, the spoon was repaired with a shallower bowl than originally intended. Despite the mishap, the lovely finish on the spoon makes the effort worthwhile.

To carve the entwined hearts, identify the points that cross under and over, just as if you were carving a Celtic knot. Angle the sides to create a camber so that each of the interlocking sections sit one on top of the other.

For a different effect, give the interlocking hearts a flat surface and right-angled edges to contrast with the rounded outer stems of the rosebud.

SIZE
Approximately 10½ x 7in (267 x 178mm)

TYPE OF WOOD

Mahogany

SYMBOLS AND MEANINGS

Rosebuds express affection.

Entwined hearts signify a love that is given and returned.

The heart-shaped bowl expresses a wish for a full and bountiful life.

MOTHER'S SPOON

This spoon was carved with much love and affection for my mother, and has a special place in my heart. It was the last gift I made for her before she died. It now hangs proudly at my sister's house and I couldn't wish for a better place for it.

Cherry is a delight to carve. Fret out the spoon with a scroll saw, ensuring a neat finish with crisp, well-defined lines.

While carving our piece, the wood was lifeless and bland, but once sanded and sealed, the rich colours just shone. Use sanding sealer to bring out the different colours in the grain of the wood of your spoon.

Shape each petal of the flowers, with one petal sitting on the other. To create these, stab cut around the pistil and around the edges of the petals that sit on top of the one below. Remove wood from the section where the petals go under others. Shape each petal so that the outer edge forms a high point and dips towards the pistil and, once done, round off the pistil/ovule to form a domed appearance. Finally, shape the leaves. Round the stems and add texture using a pyrography machine.

Carve the diamond in relief inside the section connecting the bowl and the heart. The base of the diamond must be level with the surrounding area, but you can carve a channel around the base to add definition to the shape. Form the diamond by tapering each side from the centre to the baseline on all four sides – viewed from the top it should resemble a pyramid. Slightly widen the area around the base of the diamond utilizing a triangular recess cut. To do this, stab along the edge of the diamond and, positioning your chisel at a 45–60° angle about ¹⁄₆in (0.15mm) from the stab cut, push the chisel through the wood towards the stab cut to remove the wood in a single clean cut. Slightly undercut the edge of the diamond at the baseline to throw a shadow to add emphasis to the overall effect.

SIZE
12 x 2½in (305 x 64mm)

TYPE OF WOOD
Cherry

SYMBOLS AND MEANINGS
Flowers represent affection, and this was given and returned in abundance.
Hearts represent love. A fretted heart is said to indicate a lack of real affection, but I don't think this is true. For me, a heart – regardless of shape or form – demonstrates love.
Diamonds represent wealth. Aside from literal wealth, it might indicate a wealth of love.
The heart-shaped bowl expresses a wish for a full and bountiful life.

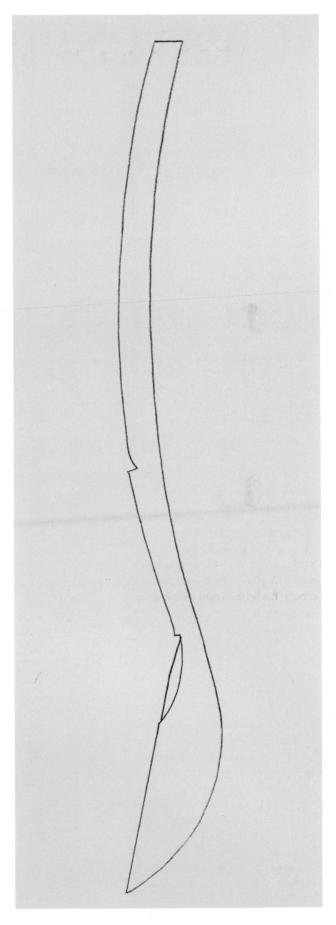

OPEN SPIRAL SPOON

This spoon came about because I wanted to create a design that was more distinctive than the others. I can honestly say that, of all the spoons I have carved, this is my favourite – it encompasses everything I like in my own or other artists' work. It is delicate, intricate, has detail and is well-balanced.

The main considerations are the open spiral (or stem) and the rings. Once the design is transferred onto the wood, remove the waste wood between the dotted lines inside the spiral loops. (The dotted lines are the back section of the spiral.) Don't do any more work on these until your spoon is virtually carved – if you work on this section too soon and exert too much pressure, the spiral may break.

An open stem or spiral was something I hadn't attempted before designing this spoon so it was a challenge but, with gentle handling and sharp chisels, it transformed the design. One drawback with an open spiral (especially if it's long) is that it creates a weak point that can break very easily so handle with care.

Fret out the area between the two interlocking hearts below the spiral, leaving the inner hearts intact so that they can be rounded to produce a cushioned effect. Shape the outer edges of the interlocking hearts to create the crossing under and over effect at the point at which they meet. Stab cut along the crossover section and remove wood at each side, gradually descending along both outer arms. Take note that the base of the smaller heart, connecting the bowl to the spoon, is set lower than the rim of the bowl.

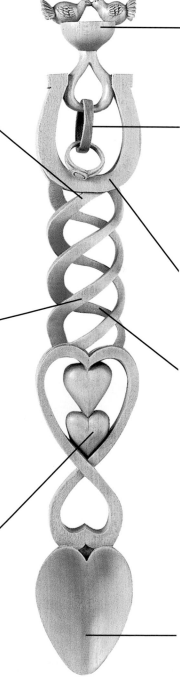

Shape the horseshoe, birds and birdbath. Carve the birds and birdbath in the round. Carve the tail and wing feathers with a knife or a chisel.

Round the section where the ring nestles. With great care, separate the rings using a knife or a very fine drill bit in a hobby drill, checking the angle all the time to avoid making holes in areas where they should not be. Once separated, work on finishing the rings.

Look at the spoon's side profile. Where the spiral connects with the horseshoe and larger fretted heart, use a knife to hollow out a segment to give the impression that two sections fuse as one (see diagram, opposite).

Work on the spiral. Slowly curve each side of the top section, then turn the spoon over and do the same with the back. The curved sides on the front and back where they meet should form a continuous flowing line along each side of the spoon. Once satisfied with the overall shape, remove the supporting wood from between the upper and lower curved sections to completely separate the spiral arms from each other. As you remove the wood, maintain the internal curve of the spiral.

The spoon has been carved in lime. This particular species of lime was very pale cream – nearly white in fact – and I like the fact that this spoon hasn't darkened with finishing products.

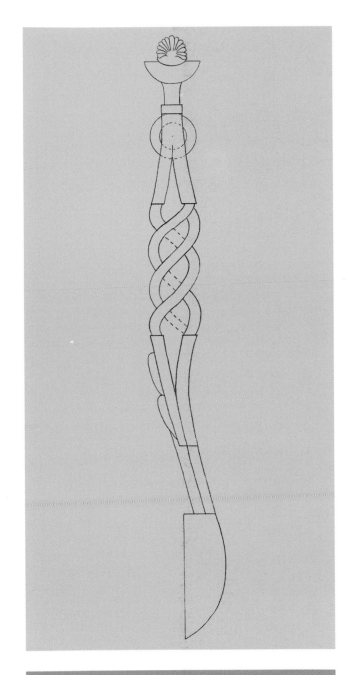

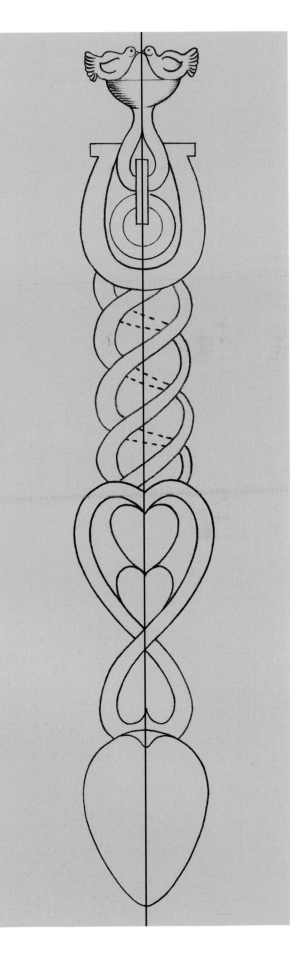

SIZE

16 x 2⅜in (406 x 61mm)

TYPE OF WOOD

Lime

SYMBOLS AND MEANINGS

The birds represent love and peace.

The rings express a desire to commit.

The horseshoe represents good luck.

The numerous hearts signify an abundance of love.

The heart-shaped bowl means a wish for a full life.

The twisted stem shows that two lives are bound by an everlasting love.

CELTIC CROSS SPOON

My nephew designed this spoon for his school art class. He chose hand-carved Welsh lovespoons as his specialist subject. Before transferring the design to wood, he first created a maquette in clay to visualize his design. The ideas were all his – and I'm biased – but I think he's transformed a traditional symbol into a modern-day equivalent. I am very proud of him.

Mark the positions for the marbles. Hollow out a small hole on the top and two outer arms so that the marbles nestle neatly into place and then glue into position.

Once you have transferred the pattern onto the wood and cut it, make vertical stab cuts around the outer edge of the circle along the two side arms and the upper arm but do not stab cut along the circle where it joins the lower arm/section of the cross. However, do make vertical stab cuts around the internal arcs of the diamond-shaped extensions on all three arms. Remove the wood from the area between the stab cuts leaving the circle and diamond extensions to stand proud.

The wood chosen for this design was beech. It is durable and able to withstand a teenager's less-than-gentle handling.

Divide the supporting lower arm into sections to create a central pillar. Stab cut along the two lines, then remove the wood from the outer sections until they are the same depth as the two side arms. Stab cut along the arc-shaped diamond inside the bowl. Shape the sides so that you form a hollowed out bowl, leaving the arced diamond virtually level with the rim of the bowl. Once satisfied that the bowl is deeply curved enough, carefully undercut the sides of the diamond so that only a thin edge is visible.

Seal and wax the spoon.

SIZE
Can vary
TYPE OF WOOD
Beech
SYMBOLS AND MEANINGS
The cross symbolizes faith in God. It also represents the joining of two people and their blessing in the eyes of God. The arc-shaped diamond is an alternative to the traditional straight-sided shape and represents good fortune. By the number of diamonds incorporated, I think my nephew is hoping for a lot of good fortune!

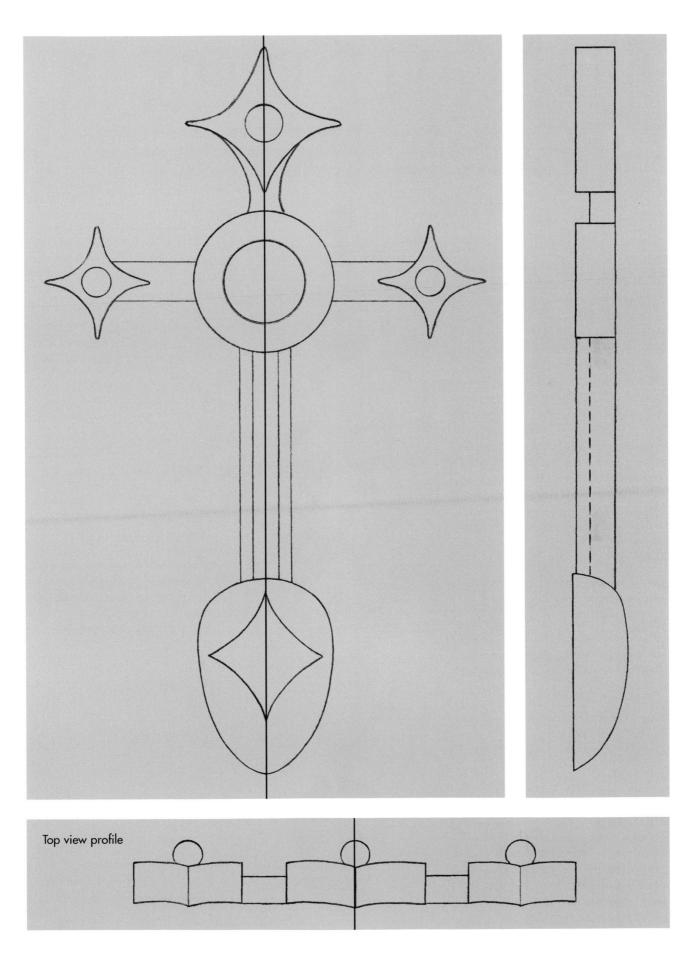

Top view profile

WAVE SPOON

This unconventional design was for a special 18th birthday. The stylized shape at the bottom, holding the heart, reminds me of a human being with his or her arms open wide, expressing joy to be alive upon 'coming of age'.

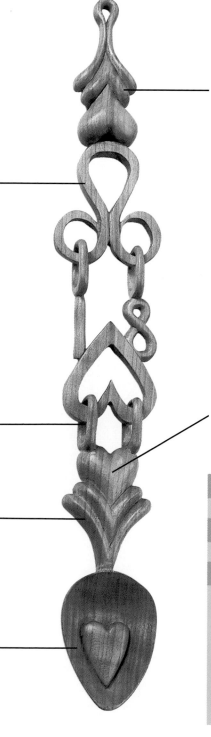

Remove waste wood from the hook shape to about half its original thickness. Take most of it from the surface on the front, but some can be removed from the back. The surface must remain flat and the curved outer circles gently taper down as they connect to the main stem of the hook. Removing this wood first makes it easier to separate the links, thus enabling the figure 18 to swing freely above the upside-down fretted heart. (For details on separating links, see page 36.) The lower links are more difficult to separate due to the inverted V of the fretted heart, but with patience you will do it – honest!

The top reversed wave narrows from the base towards the loop from which the spoon hangs. Divide it into two inverted V sections, shape them by stab cutting along the lines and rounding the edges to form a convex shape. Continue this separation along the shank towards the hanging loop, softening the sections by shallowly rounding the edges to blend with the sides.

Carved in cherry, the spoon is robust enough to withstand the manipulation required to separate the chain loops, particularly inside the fretted heart.

To cushion the heart, remove the blunt ends to create a rounded effect. Taper the base of the heart so that it is clasped within the stylized wave.

Repeat the method for the lower wave as for the one above.

Shape the bowl to about half the depth of the wood then redraw your heart into the bowl. Stab cut around the heart. Remove the remaining wood from around the heart to the desired depth while maintaining the curve of the bowl. Finally, shape the heart for a cushioned effect.

SIZE
12¾ x 1⅝in (324 x 41mm)

TYPE OF WOOD
Cherry

SYMBOLS AND MEANINGS
The hearts express steadfast love, and an abundance of affection. The links express growth, and the way destiny joins the recipient to his or her parents and/or partner. The stylized waves are a decorative feature.

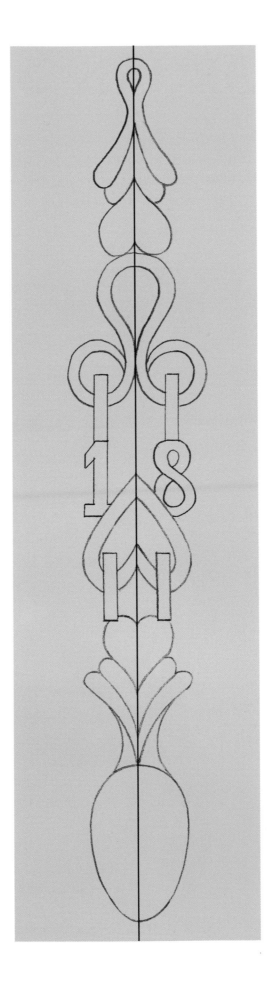

Menorcan Spoon

The design of this spoon is not Menorcan in origin, but was carved during a holiday in Menorca. It was carved using only a knife – including hollowing out the bowl of the spoon. It was pleasant sitting on the terrace whittling away with the children gathering around, asking questions.

Taper the arms on the cross from the outside edge towards the centre. For added effect, reduce the small overhang outside the outer circle of the three arms, so that they are level with the circle connecting them. Round the central section to create a dome.

I had never used eucalyptus before and found that it carved reasonably well with a knife, although it has hard parts which make work a little more difficult. One major drawback with eucalyptus is its tendency to natural internal splitting and there is no way of knowing where, when or if a split will appear. With this spoon, a long, narrow split appeared but, as luck would have it, it was on the back of the spoon which did not affect its outward appearance.

Round the solid heart hanging inside the fretted heart to create a cushioned effect.

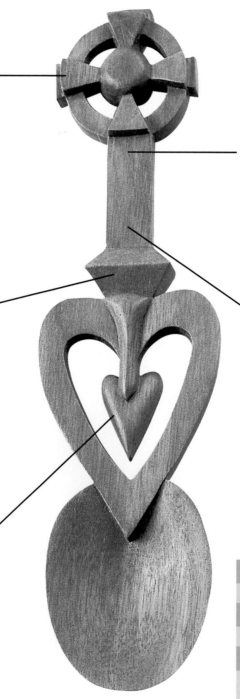

Reduce the thickness of the main stem of the cross to the same level as the outer circle. The bottom of the cross, viewed from the side, has a half-diamond effect – the central high point of which is the same level as the high point or outer edge of the arms of the cross (see the side profile). Be careful when shaping these tapered areas to maintain a straight edge along the horizontal high point – if it slants either way it will throw out the balance of the spoon.

This spoon was designed to be simple so that I might carve it on holiday with only a few tools. I took a Frost knife, a Swan Morton scalpel handle with No. 11 and No. 15 blades, and a couple of chip-carving knives. I also took some small needle files and sandpaper.

SIZE
7½ x 1¾in (191 x 44mm)

TYPE OF WOOD
Eucalyptus

SYMBOLS AND MEANINGS
A Celtic cross symbolizes faith. Hearts express love and affection.

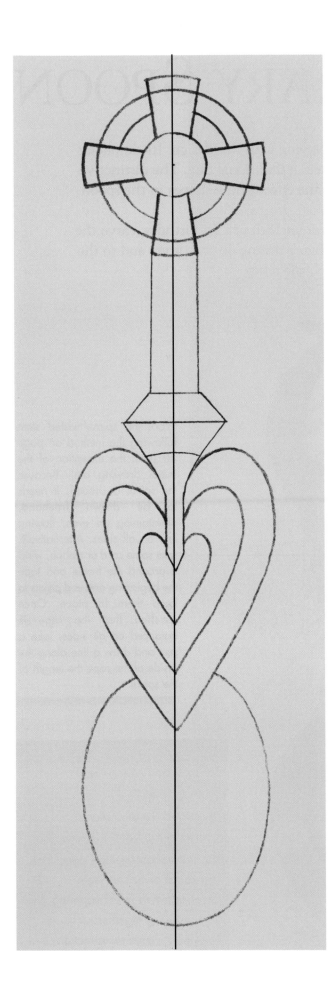

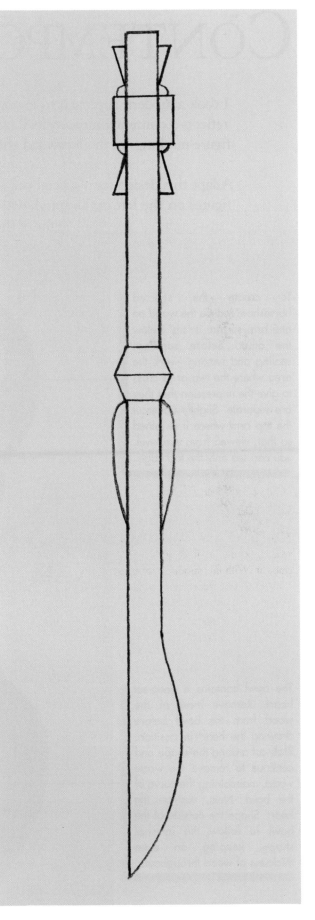

CHRISTENING SPOON

This christening spoon shows the stork gazing in adoration at the new arrival cradled in its wings. A parent remembers the details of a child's birth forever without noting them, but including these details in the spoon's design makes it an item to treasure.

I chose lime for its plain grain structure. Woods with more complex grains such as lacewood (London plane) or spalted beech would obscure the delicate detail such as the baby's face.

Before carving this, first model the shape in plasticine or clay as a visual guide. To form the baby's body, patiently remove the waste wood from the internal area of the wings until the back wing appears to curve from the tip to the other side of its body. To save shaping limbs, swaddle the baby in a blanket. The baby's face is particularly difficult to carve, so think carefully before you set the features in place.

The horseshoe sits beneath the cradle and stork. Flowers add decoration. For further details on carving flowers, see Mother's spoon, page 86.

For your own spoon, add personal details relating to a newborn infant: the baby's weight on the stork's breast, the child's name on the layette and the date of birth along the stork's wing or the base of the horseshoe. Alternatively, carve or burn the words 'Good Luck' or 'For your Christening'.

Carve the stork with a side profile of an in-the-round shape by rounding the body on each side. First shape the wings to curve into the middle of the body towards the baby. Once done, leave a small section of wood above the tip of the wing for the baby's head.

The side of the cradle gently slopes away to reveal the inside of the crib. To do this, imagine the bottom near edge of the crib is a high point and, maintaining this high point, gently remove wood towards the top edge of the crib where the curtain rests on the frame – removing more wood the closer you get to the curtain. Return to the bottom end of the crib. The intention here is to form a virtual 90° corner at the high point (the corner nearest you). To do so, remove a small amount of wood from the high point removing more as you get closer to the stork's body. Shape the curtain to look as if it drapes at all three sides. For added effect, carve a pillow and blanket inside the crib.

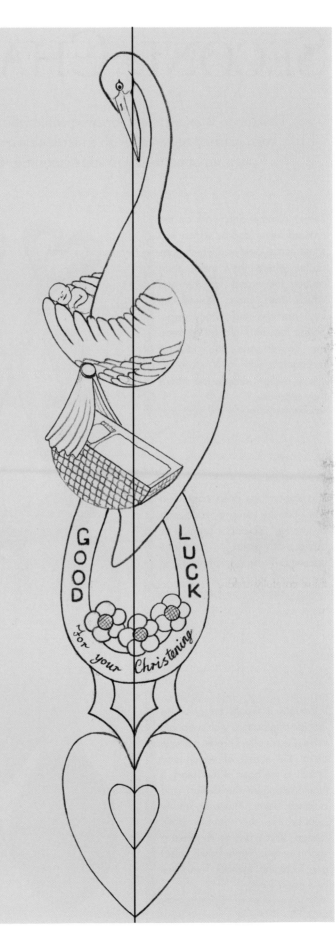

SIZE

13¼ x 2¾in (336 x 70mm)

TYPE OF WOOD

Lime

SYMBOLS AND MEANINGS

The stork represents a new arrival.
The horseshoe signifies a wish for
good luck to the child.
A heart-shaped bowl expresses a
wish for a full and bountiful life.
A heart nestled in the bowl
represents love and affection for
the child.
Flowers represent affection.

YIN AND YANG SPOON

This design was developed to attract young people to the pleasures of woodcarving. The bowl is the head of the fish and the body arched to contain the Yin and Yang symbols. The tail is exaggerated to encompass a heart.

Yin and Yang has been all the rage for some time, and appeals to young people. Yin and Yang are two complementary principles of Chinese philosophy: Yin represents the negative, dark and feminine and Yang the positive, light and masculine. Their interaction is thought to maintain the harmony of the universe (or Chi) and to influence everything within it.

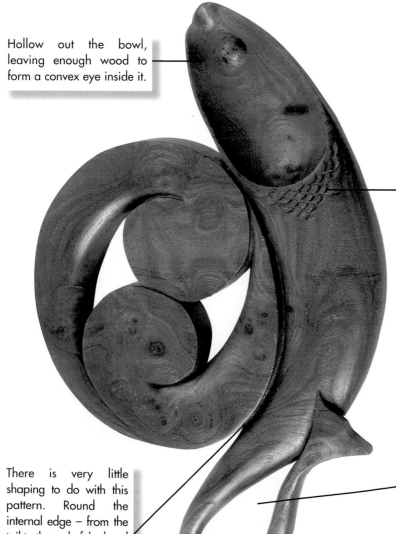

Hollow out the bowl, leaving enough wood to form a convex eye inside it.

Around the edge of the bowl and along some of the length of the body, carve a few rows of imbrications or fish scales. Fish scales are fiddly, concave scallop shapes. Take a No. 8/7 gouge and lightly position it vertically onto the wood, slightly slanting the upper part of the chisel in towards the centre of the curve with the blade remaining in its original position, then make a stab cut. Repeat this process along the row for as many rows as you require. Alternate the scallop shapes on each row, a little like laying bricks. Make sure that each stab cut meets but does not break into or overlap the edge of the previous stab cut. To make concave cuts, position one corner of a No. 7 fishtail chisel at the outer edge of the end scallop and carefully move the chisel through the wood, following the curve of the stab cut on the row below. As the point of the chisel reaches the V where the two stab cuts join, the piece of wood should come out as a complete chip. If not, sever it carefully. It may be easier to form concave cuts by making smaller cuts, but a greater quantity. If you have not done this before, try it first on a piece of waste wood.

There is very little shaping to do with this pattern. Round the internal edge – from the tail to the curl of the head of the Yin and Yang – but leave all outer edges and the edge where the heads meet at 90° angles.

Carve the heart to form a sweeping curve and, once complete, round the fish's body and where the tail rests on top of the body.

Burr elm is ideal for this pattern because of its abstract character. The twists and turns, knots and texture of the grain in the burr beautifully complement the design.

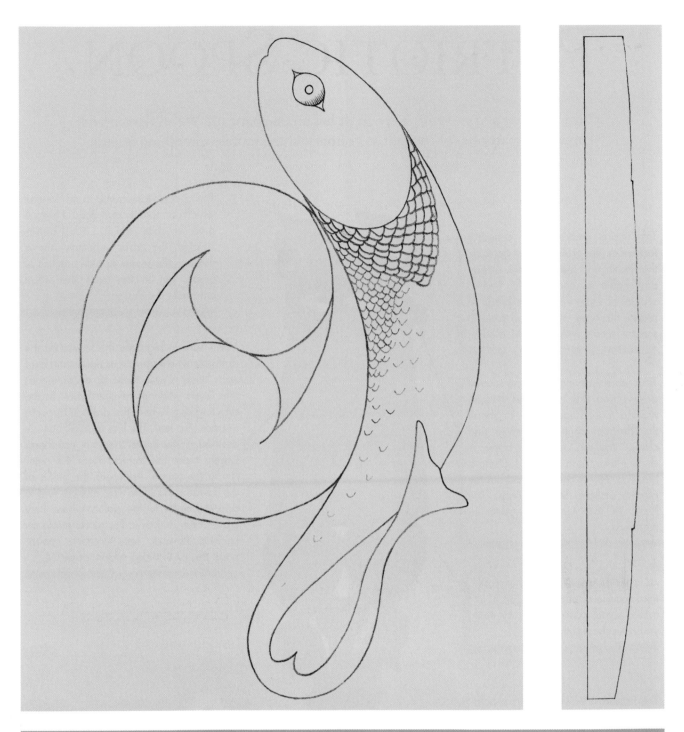

SIZE
9¾ x 7in (248 x 178mm)

TYPE OF WOOD
Burr elm

SYMBOLS AND MEANINGS
Yin and Yang represent a state of balance between interacting forces that permeates all aspects of life.
The fish is a religious symbol.
The heart inside the tail represents love of mankind, and our wish for peace and harmony irrespective of differences of sex, race and faith.

MIX & MATCH SPOON

Clive developed the design for this spoon from a concept by a friend, Derek Edwards.
Clive added to it using a selection of mix-and-match symbols,
and it has been much admired at exhibitions.

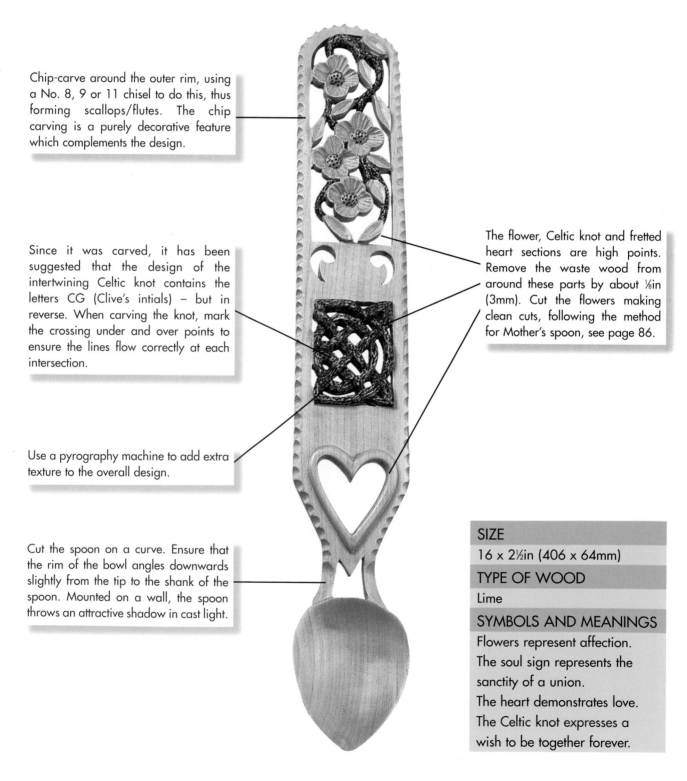

Chip-carve around the outer rim, using a No. 8, 9 or 11 chisel to do this, thus forming scallops/flutes. The chip carving is a purely decorative feature which complements the design.

Since it was carved, it has been suggested that the design of the intertwining Celtic knot contains the letters CG (Clive's intials) – but in reverse. When carving the knot, mark the crossing under and over points to ensure the lines flow correctly at each intersection.

Use a pyrography machine to add extra texture to the overall design.

Cut the spoon on a curve. Ensure that the rim of the bowl angles downwards slightly from the tip to the shank of the spoon. Mounted on a wall, the spoon throws an attractive shadow in cast light.

The flower, Celtic knot and fretted heart sections are high points. Remove the waste wood from around these parts by about ⅛in (3mm). Cut the flowers making clean cuts, following the method for Mother's spoon, see page 86.

SIZE

16 x 2½in (406 x 64mm)

TYPE OF WOOD

Lime

SYMBOLS AND MEANINGS

Flowers represent affection.
The soul sign represents the sanctity of a union.
The heart demonstrates love.
The Celtic knot expresses a wish to be together forever.

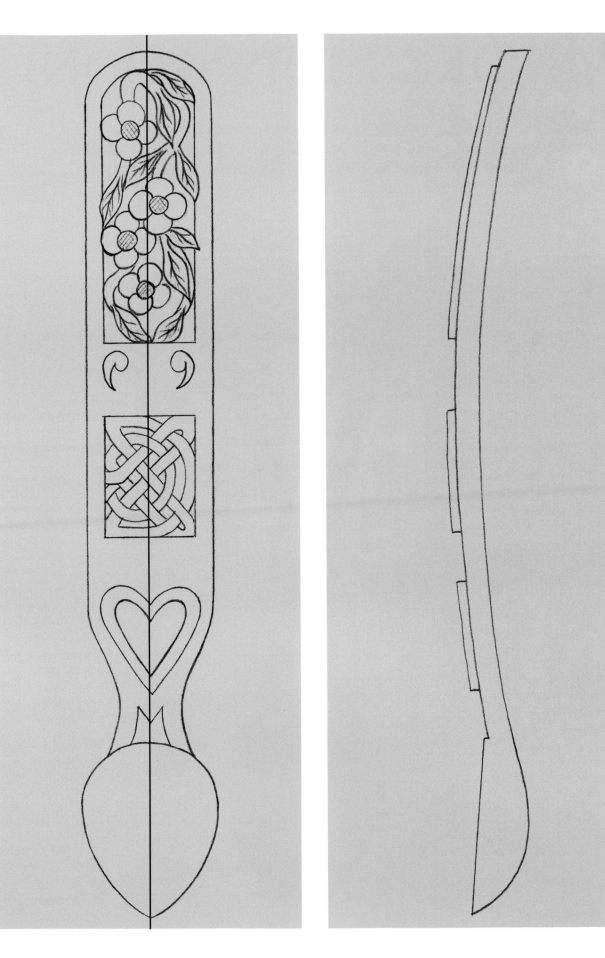

WORKSHOP SPOON

This spoon was originally designed for a two-day Welsh-themed workshop which was a great success. The students attending the workshop made the same basic spoon, but each was transofrmed by the individual's artistic vision to create twelve unique spoons.

When carving a Celtic knot, make marks with coloured pencils on the design at the crossing over and under points where you need to remove sections of wood. Use the same colour for each over or under section. Do not cut out the area where the three sections overlap. Instead, using a knife, cut a small piece from the centre. The piece that you remove is enough to separate the three interlocking sections.

Celtic knots mean never-ending love so, using a pyrograph machine, I have burnt on the back of the spoon 'A love that lasts and lasts and grows forever'. Select your own words if you wish.

If you carve the back of the spoon, look carefully at the pattern on the front side and reverse it, following the lines of the top surface so that they match on the bottom. To do this accurately, use the copy of your design, hold it up against a window (pattern to glass) with good daylight, and draw over it, then transfer this pattern onto the back of your spoon. Take your time to get it right.

Carved from the heartwood of a piece of American cherry, there is a small section of sapwood visible. The cutting out of this design is time-consuming, so use an electric scroll saw or fret saw.

The pattern is simple enough to suit a beginner, but if you want to make it more elaborate, add a heart or other motifs to the design. I've shaped the bowl into a heart shape and added a heart to the section between this and the outer rim of the bowl.

SIZE
7¾ x 4in (197 x 102mm)

TYPE OF WOOD
American cherry

SYMBOLS AND MEANINGS
Hearts represent love.
Celtic knots symbolize an everlasting love.

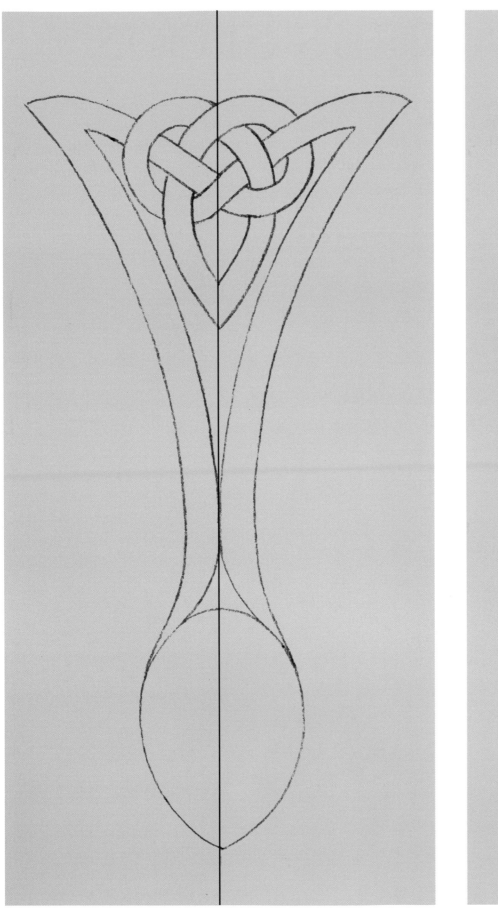

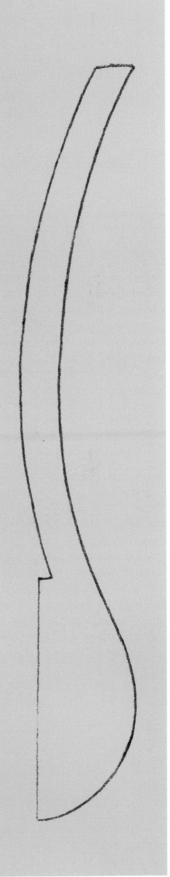

DANIEL'S SPOON

This spoon was carved for Clive's grandson. Having made a couple of spoons for his granddaughter, he felt it was about time his grandson received a handmade gift, too. Daniel was only three when this spoon was carved, so he kept the design simple. It could also be carved as an 18th birthday gift by adding a key to the central section instead of a name.

Texture the background with a home-made punch to emphasize the raised carving (see page 18).

Remove the area of wood from the lettering or motif section in the shield to the inner edge of the frame itself to a depth of ⅛in (3mm). The lettering 'Daniel' on this spoon is raised from the surface, so carefully remove wood from around each letter.

When you carve the spoon, leave the chains until last. It is easier to clamp the spoon to the bench along the chain section whilst you carve the rest of the spoon. Also, if you shape and separate the links too soon, they will catch on chisels, etc., and you are more likely to break them. For further details on carving chains and links, see page 36.

Finish the spoon with sanding sealer and wax.

SIZE
16¾ x 3in (424 x 76mm)

TYPE OF WOOD
Lime

SYMBOLS AND MEANINGS
The heart expresses love.
The heart-shaped bowl represents a wish for a full and bountiful life.
Chains mean a wish to be linked to loved ones.

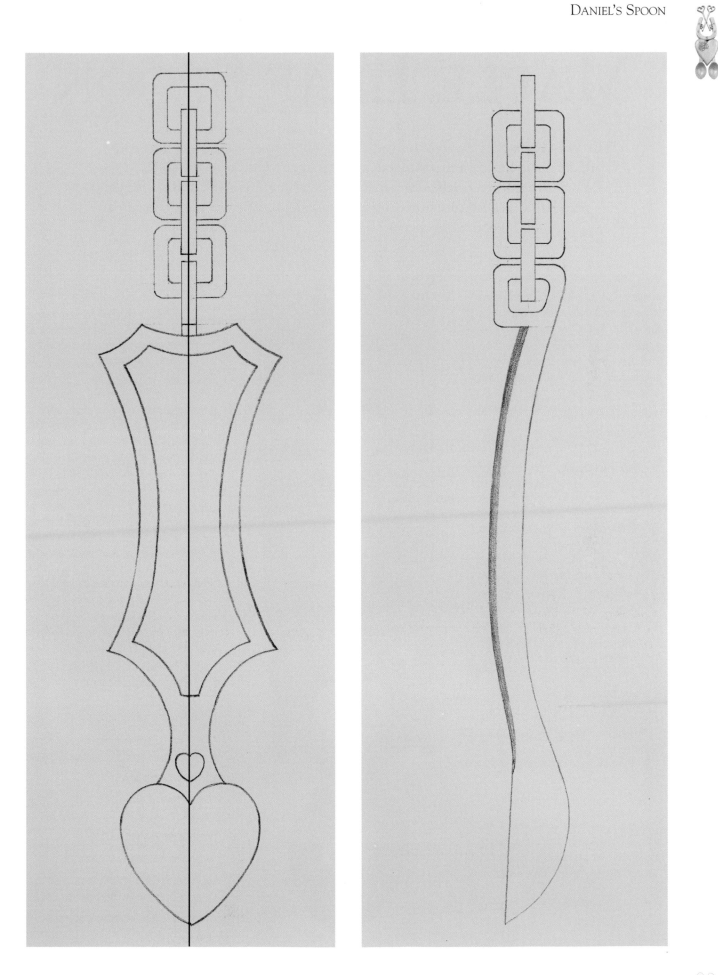

MAPLE LEAF SPOON

Clive carved this spoon for the parents of his daughter-in-law. They are Canadian so he incorporated a maple leaf motif. The father-in-law is in the lumber trade, so Clive added an axe in honour of his skill. These touches personalize a spoon and make it a meaningful gift. The outline shape of this spoon was borrowed from a design by Mike Davies.

Carve the overlapping petals in a similar way to Mother's spoon (see page 86). Remove the wood from the outer edges of the flowers to emphasize the depth. To help you visualize how they should look in relief, take a cup and saucer and view it from above.

Curve the back to create shadow on the wall.

The maple leaf must be joined to the main panel of wood at the stem. When you cut the outline of the leaf, take extra care not to apply too much pressure to this small section of wood. While the grain runs lengthways (which makes it slightly stronger) it is still susceptible to breakage.

Slightly bevel the edges of the hollowed out hearts to achieve a rounded effect.

When you work the bowl, angle the shape downwards from the tip of the spoon to the shank, to cast a nice shadow when mounted on the wall.

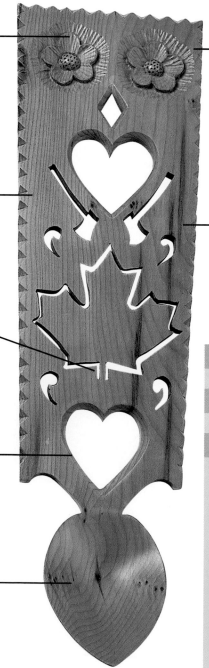

Yew has a beautiful grain and lends itself well to lovespoon carving. A slight drawback is its tendency to split and chip.

Before chip carving the edges, mark the length of your wood into equal divisions to evenly space the cuts. Using a knife or chisel held at a 45° angle to the corner, slice from the outer edge of the cut towards the centre of the marked section, then move your knife to the other side of the mark and cut from that edge inwards to the centre so that the wood chips cleanly away.

SIZE
13¼ x 4in (336 x 102mm)

TYPE OF WOOD
Yew

SYMBOLS AND MEANINGS
The flowers express Clive's regard for his in-laws.
The heart expresses love.
The maple leaf is the national emblem of Canada, and reflects the family's roots.
Soul signs represent the sanctity of a union. They usually appear in pairs, and resemble nostrils, through which the soul is said to escape at death.

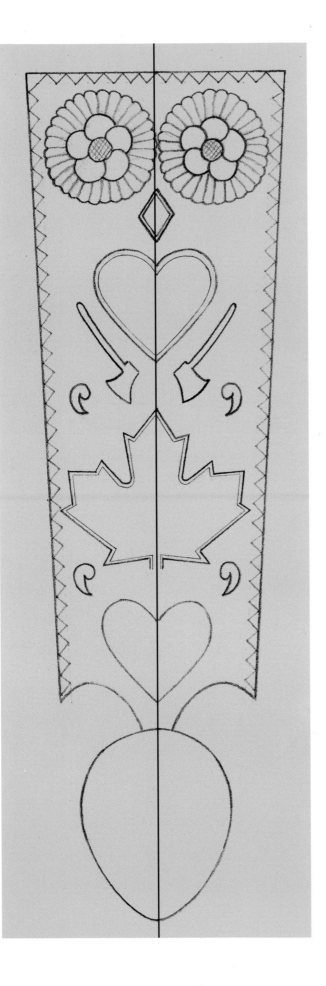

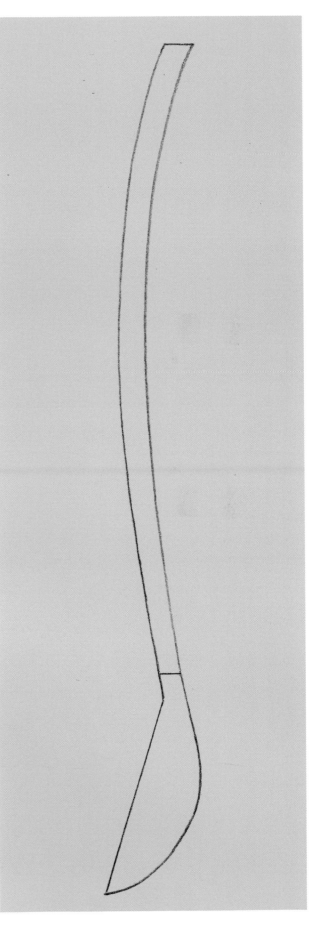

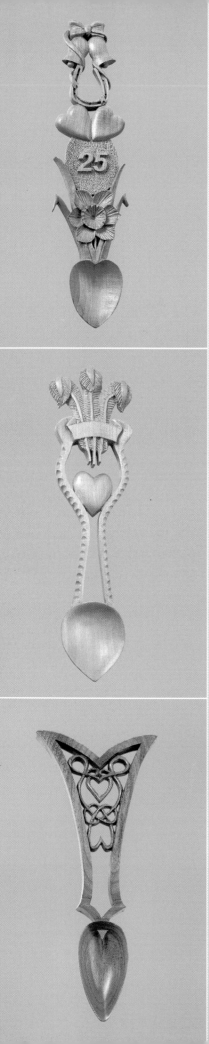
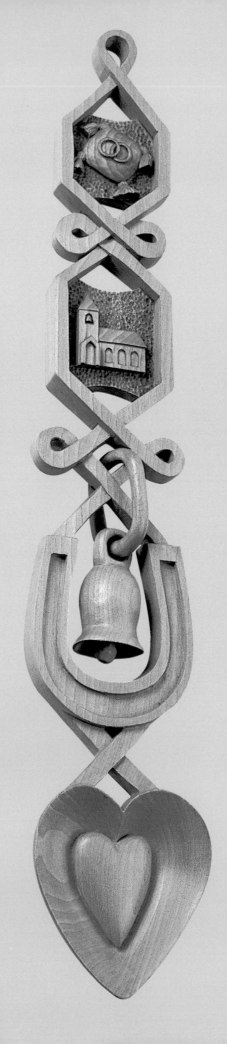
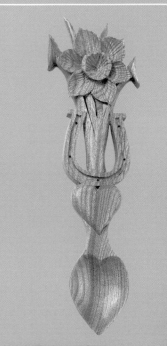

APPENDIX

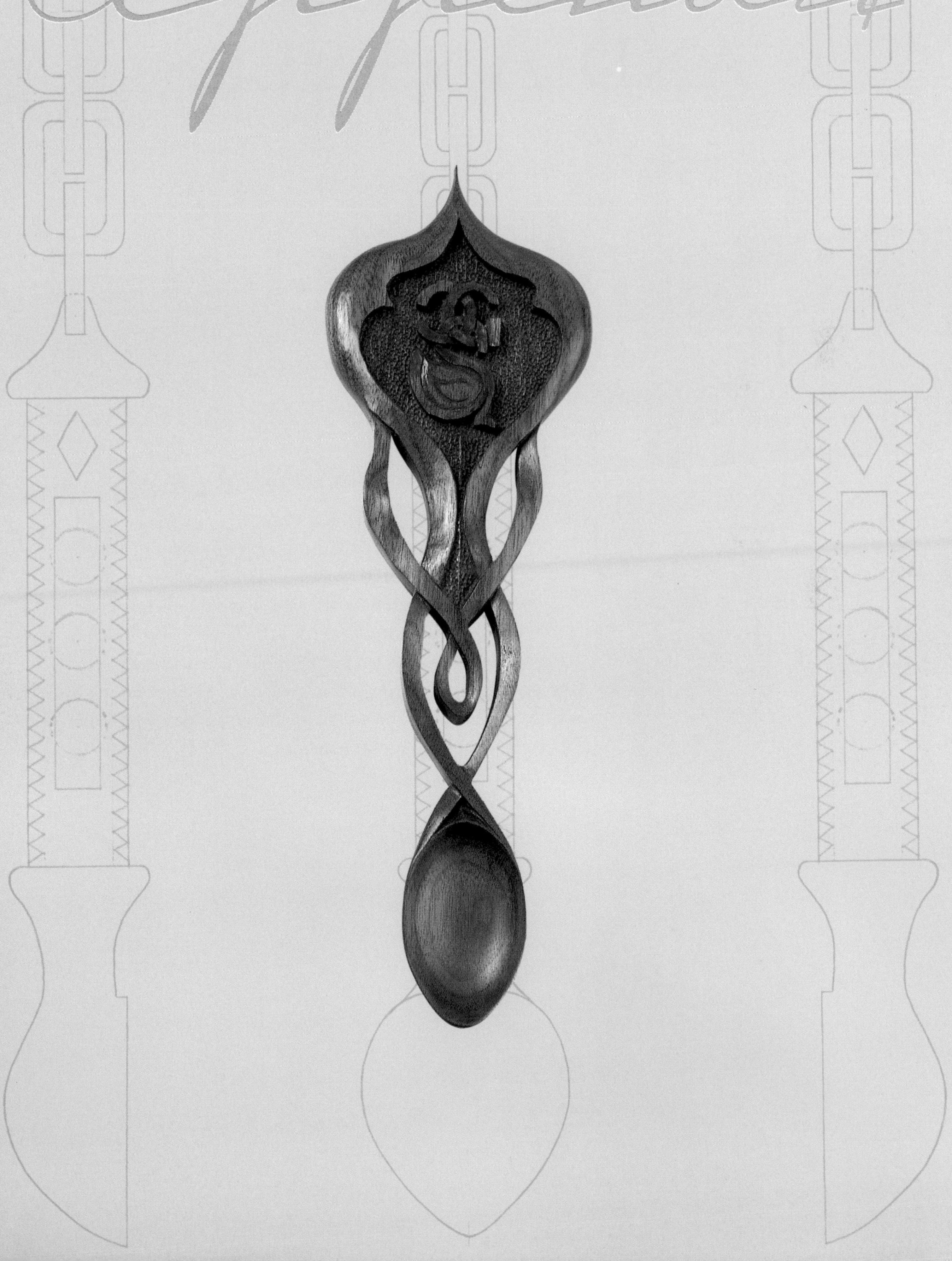

QUESTIONS
AND ANSWERS

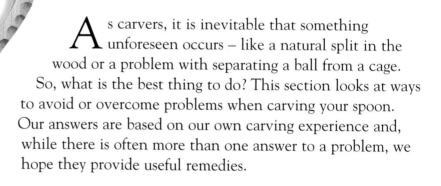

As carvers, it is inevitable that something unforeseen occurs – like a natural split in the wood or a problem with separating a ball from a cage. So, what is the best thing to do? This section looks at ways to avoid or overcome problems when carving your spoon. Our answers are based on our own carving experience and, while there is often more than one answer to a problem, we hope they provide useful remedies.

How do you make a pattern the same shape and size on one side of the spoon as the other?

There are a number of ways of doing this, but this is one of the easiest. Draw a line down the centre of a piece of paper. On one side of the line draw one half of your pattern, making sure you gauge the size of each symbol to balance the overall design. Once done, fold the paper along the central line, keeping the drawing uppermost, cut around the outline of the half of the design you have drawn. As you do so, be careful to keep the two halves pressed together so that both sides of the design match. Cut out internal fretted areas. Unfold the paper and you will have a perfect pattern.

Make a photocopy of the design, or draw around the outline on a fresh sheet of paper so that you have a copy of the original for your own reference.

Once I have cut out the front profile of a spoon, how do I draw and cut out the side profile if I don't have a flat surface on which to transfer the shape, and to place on the saw bench?

If your spoon has, for example, a curved handle, it can be difficult to cut this out on a bandsaw, especially if the side edges of your design are uneven. One way to overcome this is to cut out the front profile on a scroll saw in one piece if possible, reserving the cut-off

sections. Remove any internal areas of waste wood before moving on. Reposition each cut-off side piece, securing firmly into place with masking tape. Draw the side profile along one of the repositioned sides of the spoon. Next, using the bandsaw, place the other side onto the saw table and cut along the marked line. Keep this cut-off curved section as a support piece for when you are working on the spoon (see page 27 for further details).

Is there an easy way to avoid making mistakes when carving a Celtic knot?

A Celtic knot forms a single, continuous line that crosses under and over itself. As a series of lines on a flat surface, it can be difficult to see where the crossings occur. One way to identify which is which is to look at the line: if at the crossover juncture the line continues, this is the 'over', but if the line comes to an abrupt end with a gap and continues beyond, this is the 'under'. It is easy enough to make a mistake but, to avoid doing so, always make a mark on your work so that you can see where you are at a glance if you are interrupted. I use a red dot to indicate a crossing over and a blue dot for a crossing under. Making marks in this way will save you spoiling your work and wasting time.

I've separated the ball from its cage too soon and there is work still to be finished – what can I do?

Don't worry, there are ways to overcome the problem. Holding the ball in position and shaping it at the same time is inadvisable, but possible. Wedge rubber erasers into each side of the ball to hold it in place. If this doesn't work, try inserting as much Blu-Tack as required into the cage to cradle the ball in place. Make sure to remove every bit of Blu-Tack afterwards. This should allow you to continue with your work.

How can I get into awkward areas when sanding my work?

Sanding is the bane of every carver's life. Sanding is a treat for me as it's the only time I get to watch TV (or rather – hear it – since I'm busy sanding) – but at least the job seems much quicker and, since I am the one who does the housework, I don't nag myself about getting dust everywhere!

To make the task easier, there are numerous aids available to buy or make yourself from everyday household objects. Double-sided sticky tape is essential for this task. Use it to adhere wax modelling tools, dentists' tools and off-cuts of wood to pieces of sandpaper to access those awkward areas. I have an item made of rubber – originally part of a horse's reins – which is long and narrow with oval end pieces onto which I attach sandpaper. This allows me to apply more pressure when sanding curved areas. Other objects – pens, pencils, skewers, knitting needles, etc. – adhered to sandpaper are also extremely easy-to-make and useful tools, especially for forming a barley twist. A tool we strongly recommend for the barley twist is a Perma-Grit round file – it's better than any other option.

Sanding drums and domed heads that fit into flexible shaft machines make light of sanding these areas. They are extremely useful for sanding lovespoon bowls: drums are great for convex shapes and domed heads for concave shapes.

Another useful aid for smoothing work is a scraper. On smaller areas of work I find the more pliable clay-modelling scrapers are best. The burr on one edge of the scraper removes quantities of wood much quicker than sanding. To create a burr, mount the scraper into a vice, take a metal bar – a screwdriver, chisel or something made of tougher steel than the scraper – and rub the steel along the edge of the scraper at a slight angle. This pushes enough metal over the edge of the scraper to form a burr (or turned edge). To test it, gently run your finger over the edge. Old bandsaw blades or hacksaw blades cut to shape make good scrapers, too, and conform to the recycling trend. To use a scraper, hold it at a 60–90° angle to the wood with the burred edge facing you and pull it towards you.

Whichever method you choose, always work along the grain of the wood, and be sure to remove all cuts and scratches from your wood, or they will stand out against the rest of the wood when you apply shellac, oil or wax.

What can I do about splits or breakages in the spoon?

There are a number of solutions. When you buy wood, and before you transfer your design, check for natural splits in the wood (or 'shakes' as they are commonly known). If you see any, discard the end piece and start from further down the length of wood.

If the wood develops splits as you work – which can happen if the wood has not dried sufficiently – one answer is to apply glue to the area and clamp it until secure. This solution will be abhorrent to the purists, as the principle of carving a lovespoon is to use a single piece of wood, but it saves you rejecting all your hard work. If the crack is slightly too wide, another option is to fill it with sawdust from the same wood mixed with glue. The disadvantage of this method is that the glue darkens the sawdust, thereby leaving a distinct

line on the surface of your piece. I once carved a spoon in eucalyptus where this occured, and I am thankful that it did not appear on the front of the spoon, as the sawdust and glue filler is much darker than the wood.

You can also use wax filler sticks (available from a company called Liberon in a multitude of colours). Slice off thin slivers of this block of hard wax and work it between fingers and thumb until soft and malleable, like plasticine. With a wax filler tool, push the wax into the split as far as possible, and then carefully level it to a smooth surface.

Finally, keep offcuts of wood to plug the offending gap. This is less likely to be appropriate when carving lovespoons but is a possibility in other styles of carving such as in-the-round.

How can I ensure my work looks the way I visualize it beforehand?

First, find as much reference material – books, plastic animals, models, photographs, figurines – as possible. Look at objects you would like to copy. Keep them by your side as you work and refer to them constantly.

Alternatively, use plasticine or wax modelling clay. By moulding the shape you want (and studying reference material), you should begin to get a feel for what it is you are aiming for, and your work will improve the more you do it. And look at your work from different angles. Look at the image with a mirror as you hold it. Studying the shape like this helps you see what you need to do to put it right.

Exercise your drawing skills. You may feel that you are no good at it, but one thing is certain – the more you practise, the better you'll become. Some people are natural artists, and drawing is second nature to them – I admire and envy those people – but for others, it is a skill that can be acquired with practice and is well worth the effort.

SYMBOL TEMPLATES

We are often told by carvers that they are unable to draw, which makes designing spoons difficult for them. Please refer to this section when creating your own unique designs – there are a wide selection of symbols and motifs for you to use as templates or copy by hand for your own designs. If you wish, you can also adapt the symbols and motifs included here, or make up your own to create your unique carved lovespoons.

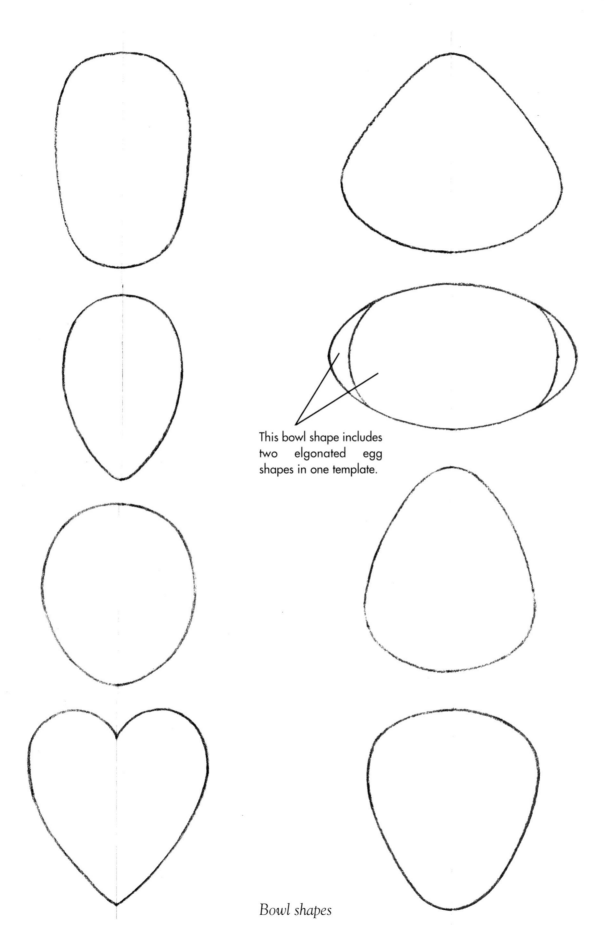

This bowl shape includes two elgonated egg shapes in one template.

Bowl shapes

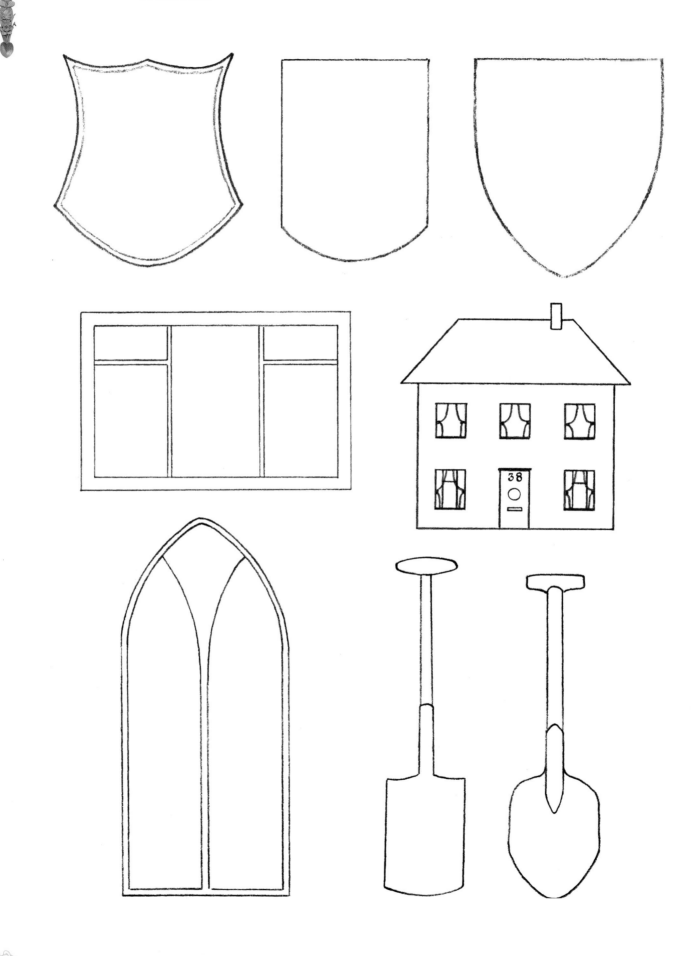

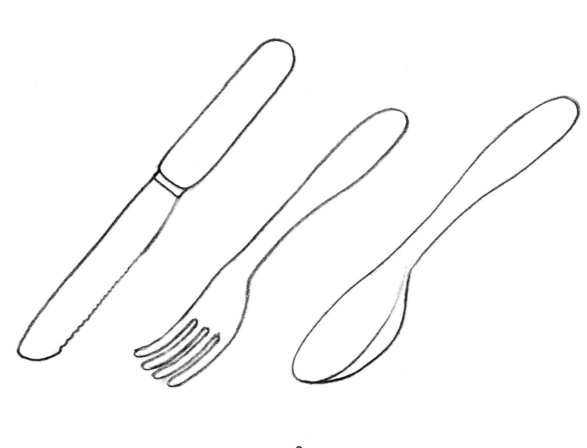

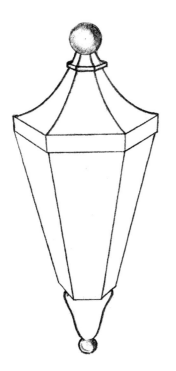

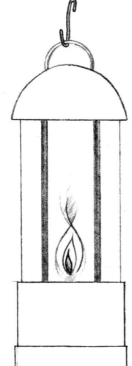

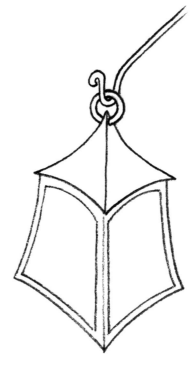

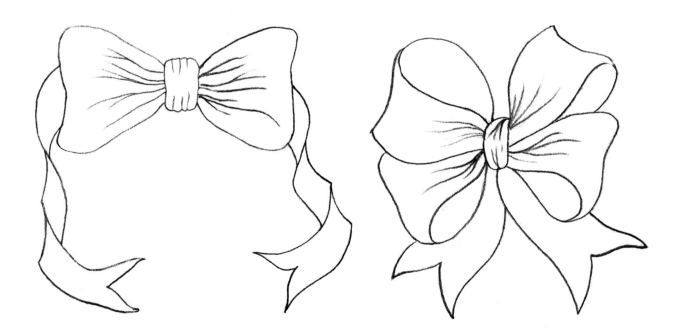

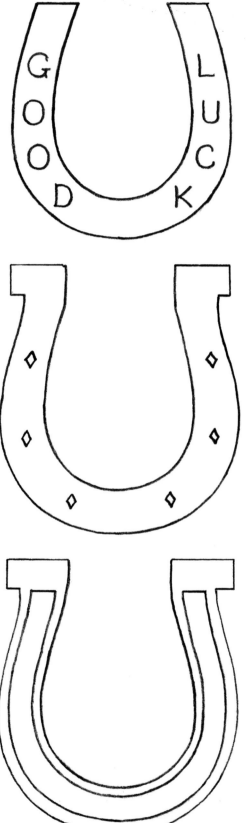

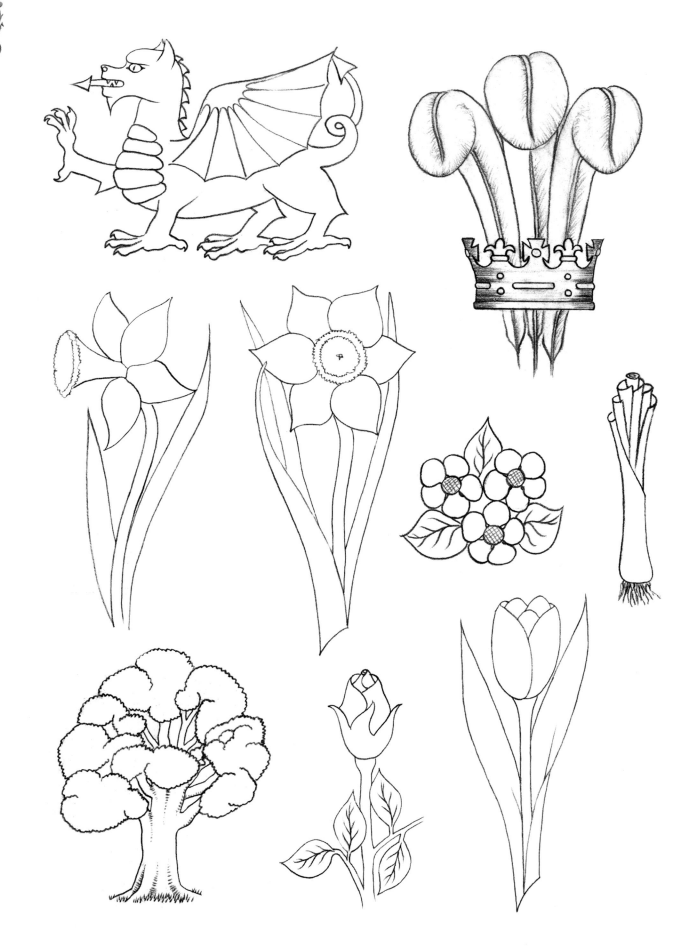

SUPPLIERS AND SOURCES OF INFORMATION

MAIL ORDER SUPPLIERS

UK

Data Power Tools
Michaelstown Road
Culverhouse Cross
Cardiff
Wales
Tel: 02920–595710

Axminster Power Tools
Chard Street
Axminster
Devon, EX13 5DZ
England
Tel: 0800–371822
Website: www.axminster.co.uk

Isca Hardwoods
c/o Paul Roberts, Timber Sales
4 Tredegar Terrace
Risca, NP11 6BY
Wales
Tel: 01633–614585

Fiddes & Son Ltd
Brindley Road
Cardiff
Wales
Tel: 02920–340323

Pintail Carving
20 Sheppenhall Grove
Aston
Nantwich
Cheshire, CW5 8DF
England
Tel: 01270–780056

Tilgear
Bridge House
Station Road
Cuffley
Hertfordshire
England
Tel: 01707–873434

John Boddy's Fine Wood & Tool Store
Riverside Sawmills
Boroughbridge
Yorkshire
England
Tel: 01423–322370

Craft Supplies
The Mill
Millers Dale
Buxton
Derbyshire
England
Tel: 01298–871636

Liberon Waxes Ltd
Mountfield Industrial Estate
New Romney
Kent, NP28 8XU
England
Tel: 01797–367555

Ashley Iles (Edge Tools) Ltd
East Kirkby
Spilsby
Lincolnshire, PE23 4DD
England
Tel: 01790–763372
Email: sales@ashleyiles.co.uk

Yandles & Sons Ltd
Hurst Works
Martock
Somerset
England
Tel: 01935–822207

USA

Mountain Woodcarvers
150 East Riverside Dr.
PO Box 3485
Estes Park
Colorado 80517
Tel: 1 (303) 586 8678
Website: www.mountaincarvers.com

Rick & Ellen Butz
PO Box 151
Blue Mountain Lake
NY 128112
Tel: 1 (518) 352 7737

Woodcraft Supply Corp.
210 Wood County Ind. Park
PO Box 1686
Parkerburg
WV 26102
Tel: 1 (304) 464 5286

MUSEUMS

Museum of Welsh Life
St Fagans
Cardiff, CF5 6XB
Wales
Tel: 01222–569441

Brecknock Museum and Art Gallery
Captain's Walk
Brecon
Powys, LD3 7DW
Wales
Tel: 01874–624121

BOOKS

Pye, Chris
Woodcarving, Tools, Materials and Equipment
GMC Publications Ltd, Lewes, East Sussex
ISBN 1 86108 201 0 (Vol I) and 202 9 (Vol 2)

Onians, Dick
Essential Woodcarving Techniques
GMC Publications Ltd, Lewes, East Sussex
ISBN 1 86108 042 5

WORKSHOPS

UK

Sharon Littley
Heartwood School of Woodcarving
Email: sha.heartwood@tinyworld.co.uk
        sha.heartwood@ukonline.co.uk

USA

Wayne Barton
Alpine School of Woodcarving
225 Vine Ave.
Park Ridge
IL 60068
Tel: 1 (708) 692 2822

GALLERY

Sharon's very first piece of carving, 1989.

Sharon's second spoon, carved as a token to celebrate her parents' life together until her father's death in 1986, was made for her mother.

Sharon's third carving, which won Silver medal at the National Woodworkers' Show in London, 1994.
Originally designed for her sister, it quickly became a spoon to keep for herself
– but has been left to her sister in her will, instead!

Sharon made this spoon for her aunt and uncle to celebrate their Golden Anniversary, 1997.

*A commissioned spoon. The request was for a design incorporating a Celtic knot,
entwined hearts, crossed keys and chains, and this is the result.*

Sharon carved this spoon as a commission for a wedding present. The bride is French but has Welsh blood, and both bride and groom love rugby, hence the rugby balls.

This spoon was carved for a friend in bed one night with only the light of a bedside lamp and a knife. The hand symbolizes my offering of friendship. As you can see, the spoon is tiny – barely as long as a matchstick.

Spoon carved by Clive for his granddaughter – he asked for an easy pattern and this was the result!

This spoon was carved by Clive. The flowers express an abundance of affection.

Clive carved this spoon as a heirloom to pass on to his children, and to their children. It was based on a design first seen in a book by W E Williams. It was carved in yew and has a rich reddish gold lustre. The balls in a cage represent his three sons, and their initials and years of birth have been carved into each one. This took him quite some time to carve, but it was well worth the effort.

Celtic knot lovespoon carved by Clive.

A second Celtic knot spoon carved by Clive.

Clive made this spoon for his granddaughter. He has added a link to celebrate each year of her life.
(There are seven links and the loop to which they are attached, making eight in total.)

ABOUT THE AUTHORS

A native of Bridgend in South Wales, **Sharon Littley** worked for 25 years in office administration, but now teaches adult education classes in woodcarving and computer studies. Primarily a self-taught carver, Sharon is currently enrolled on a City & Guilds woodcarving course led by highly respected woodcarver, Dick Onians. Now semi-professional, she has a successful small business, Heartwood, which runs workshops and fulfils commissions.

She has been invited by the Welsh Tourist Board and National Assembly to promote traditional Welsh lovespoon carving abroad. In partnership with student, co-author and valued friend Clive Griffin, they have exhibited and demonstrated carving worldwide.

Clive Griffin was born in Neath, also in South Wales. He trained and was employed as a carpenter and joiner. He later switched to a career with BP but was forced to retire early due to ill health. He now carves for enjoyment, assisting Sharon with her business when he can. He is thrilled to be involved with this book.

INDEX

More Great Project Books from Fox Chapel Publishing

Carving Spoons by Shirley Adler: Carve beautiful Welsh love spoons and Celtic knots with the 23 full-size patterns in this book. Features two start-to-finish demonstrations plus a history of spoon making. ISBN: 1-56523-092-2, 75 pages, soft cover, $14.95.

Carving Signs by Greg Krockta and Roger Schroeder: The woodworker's complete guide to carving, lettering and gilding signs. Includes lettering techniques and styles, full-color photographs and gallery, and a special chapter on gold leafing. ISBN: 1-56523-131-7, 128 pages, soft cover, $19.95.

Lettercarving in Wood: A comprehensive guide to the art and craft of lettercarving. Covers essential background information on tolls, woods and working drawings; then moves forward to step-by-step demonstrations and exercises on incised and raised lettering. Includes 37 exercises and 9 projects plus 5 commonly used alphabets. ISBN: 1-56523-210-0, soft cover, $19.95.

Step-by-Step Relief Carving by Dave Bennett and Roger Schroeder: Learn the secrets to successful relief carving with the step-by-step instruction in this book. Special emphasis on using light to create shadows and depth included. ISBN: 1-56523-101-5, 80 pages, soft cover, $17.95.

Carving Realistic Flowers in Wood by Wanda Marsh: Three projects, each incorporating new skills and techniques, are structured to guide you through the basics of flower carving. Includes reference photos, full-size patterns and step-by-step demonstrations for the morning glory, the hibiscus and the rose. ISBN: 1-56523-154-6, 64 pages, soft cover, $17.95.

Whittling Twigs and Branches by Chris Lubkemann: A knife and a little know-how is all you need to turn simple twigs into miniature wonders! Learn basic curling techniques required to create flowers, roosters and more. Perfect for beginning and experienced whittlers! ISBN: 1-56523-149-X, 64 pages, soft cover, $9.95.

Call 800-457-9112 or visit us on the web at www.foxchapelpublishing.com to order!